Glass Painting
for the first time®

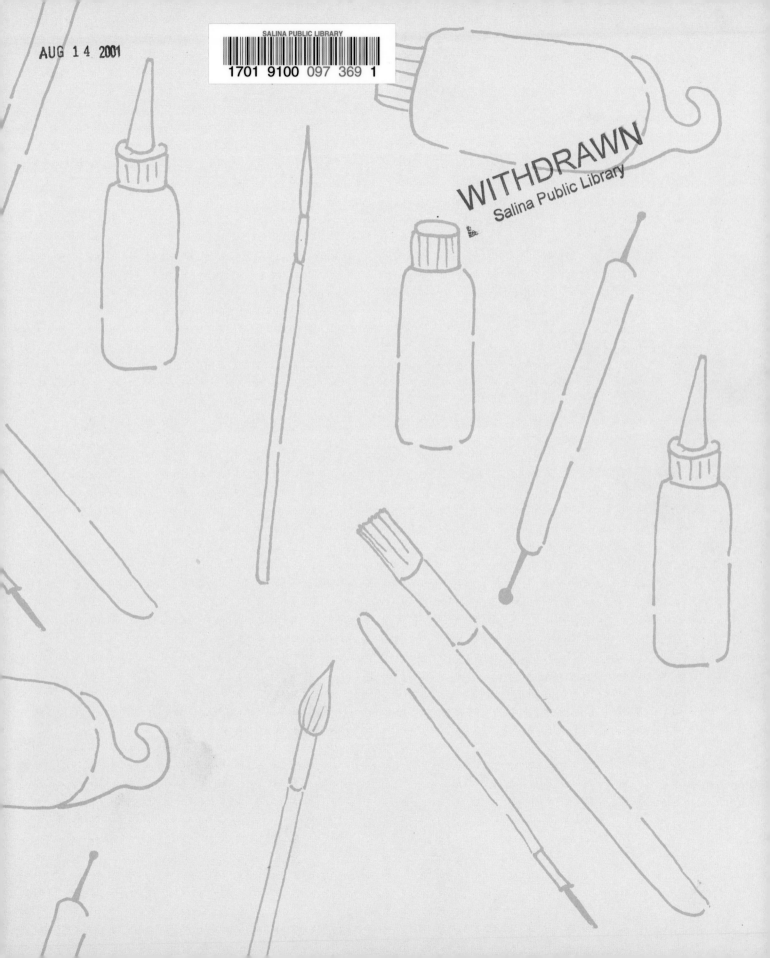

Glass Painting
for the first time®

Dorris Sorensen

Sterling Publishing Co., Inc.
New York
A Sterling/Chapelle Book

Chapelle Ltd.

Owner: Jo Packham

Editor: Leslie Ridenour

Staff: Areta Bingham, Kass Burchett, Marilyn Goff, Holly Hollingsworth, Susan Jorgensen, Kimberly Maw, Barbara Milburn, Linda Orton, Karmen Quinney, Cindy Stoeckl, Gina Swapp, Kim Taylor, Sara Toliver, Kristi Torsak

Project photography: Kevin Dilley for Hazen Photography

Special Thanks

I would like to dedicate this book to Billie Worrell and Barbie Vasek, you've both been such good listeners. I couldn't ask for a better support team. You've both exercised more patience with me than I could ever hope to repay. Even though you may not be aware of it, you both have been very instrumental in the completion of this book. Also, a special thank you to Marie Browning and Tracia Ledford Williams for their encouraging words of, "Absolutely, go ahead and just do it!"

Library of Congress Cataloging-in-Publication Data

Sorensen, Dorris.
   Glass painting for the first time / Dorris Sorensen.
      p. cm.
   "A Sterling/Chapelle book."
   Includes index.
   ISBN 0-8069-8731-6
   1. Glass painting and staining--Technique. I. Title.
NK5410 .S67 2001
748.5'28'2--dc21

2001020115

A Sterling/Chapelle Book

Published by Sterling Publishing Company, Inc.
387 Park Avenue South, New York, NY 10016
© 2001 by Dorris Sorensen
Distributed in Canada by Sterling Publishing
% Canadian Manda Group, One Atlantic Avenue, Suite 105
Toronto, Ontario, Canada M6K 3E7
Distributed in Great Britain and Europe by Cassell PLC
Wellington House, 125 Strand, London WC2R 0BB, England
Distributed in Australia by Capricorn Link (Australia) Pty Ltd.
P.O. Box 6651, Baulkham Hills, Business Centre, NSW 2153, Australia
Printed in China

Sterling ISBN 0-8069-8731-6

Due to the limited amount of space available, we must print our patterns at a reduced size in order to give our patrons the maximum number of patterns possible in our publications. We believe the quality and quantity of our patterns will compensate for any inconvenience this may cause.

Every effort has been made to ensure that all of the information in this book is accurate. However, due to differing conditions, tools, and individual skills, the publisher cannot be responsible for any injuries, losses, and/or any other damages which may result from the use of the information in this book.

If you have any questions or comments, please contact:

Chapelle Ltd., Inc.
P.O. Box 9252
Ogden, UT 84409
Phone: (801) 621-2777
FAX: (801) 621-2788
e-mail: Chapelle@chapelleltd.com
website: www.chapelleltd.com

About the Author

Dorris Sorensen hadn't even held a paintbrush until after her children were in Jr. High school. At that point she decided that she would sign up for a tole painting class at a local studio. After that, she was off and running and has never looked back. She is a prime example that anyone can paint.

Dorris has enjoyed every facet of the decorative-painting industry. She started as a student and immediately turned to teaching to pay for more classes. She has been a teacher for the past 25 years. For 15 years she owned and operated her own decorative-paint and wood shop. This was a most exciting time for her, as she not only was the shop owner but taught most of the classes offered in her shop. She has taught beginning, intermediate, and advanced decorative-painting classes. She still teaches classes for Delta® Technical Coatings at the major trade and decorative-painting shows. She feels the fun part of teaching is being able to share everything you know with your students and watching them grow as their abilities advance.

She has also spent several years as a professional crafter and has sold her painted designs at the Dallas Gift Market and Los Angeles Gift Market. This was a family business, which included her son and daughter-in-law. It was a delightful experience as they found their items sold extremely well.

Dorris has appeared on several national television programs, including Many Facets of Crafting, The Carol Duvall Show, Home Matters, and Aleene's Creative Living Show. She feels that appearing on TV is just another dimension of teaching. Of course, she has done this for so many years that she feels perfectly comfortable with it and enjoys every minute of it.

Much of Dorris's time is spent writing various craft and decorative-painting articles for numerous national magazines. She has been authoring books almost from the day she started painting. To date, she has authored 36 various publications covering all the different areas of the craft and decorative-painting market. She feels that the various experiences she has had have been instrumental in helping her to become a better designer and author.

A member of the Delta Design Force for the past nine years, Dorris is also an active member of the Society of Craft Designers and a member of The Society of Decorative Painters. She resides in Oklahoma where she and her husband Howard have lived for the past five years. They have an 80-acre farm where her husband raises registered quarter horses and where Dorris enjoys watching and feeding a menagerie of wild animals, including turkeys, deer, raccoons, numerous birds, squirrels, and rabbits. She has even had a couple of visits from a very curious bobcat. She also has a pet donkey whose name is Teddy Bear and who is an absolute delight.

Dorris has two children and eight grandchildren. Although she doesn't live near them any longer, she enjoys having them all for summer visits and, whenever possible, attending their ball games, recitals, and other activities.

Table of Contents

Section 3: Projects Beyond the Basics   58

Section 4: Gallery of Artists   90

Glass painting for the first time

Introduction

Welcome to the wonderful world of glass painting. I am so excited to be able to share this fun and exciting hobby with you. It can be as simple as sponging on a little paint to make a fun and funky design or as involved as painting some of the intricate designs that you will learn how to complete through the various techniques and projects in this book.

There is something for everyone. Glass painting is a hobby that can be done at any age. It can be a wonderful craft for children. Just a little supervision is needed for a child to enjoy this fun painting experience. Crafters of all ages will enjoy the creativity that can be unleashed in them. All you need is a few paintbrushes and a few bottles of paint and you are ready to start.

Glass painting is a fun and functional hobby. You can paint on so many different and versatile surfaces. You will be amazed at the things that are just lying around your house and that make wonderful surfaces for painting. Look in your cupboards and even the refrigerator. Take a mismatched set of glasses or dishes, paint the same design on each piece in coordinating colors, and you instantly have a matching set. An overlooked pickle jar can become a delightful treasure for gift giving. Paint on a simple design, add a bow, fill the jar with goodies, and you have a fun gift for just a few cents.

Glass paints are a wonderful way to keep up with the newest trends of home decor. You can paint anything, from the smallest vase to the largest mirrors and shower doors. Just remember that various brands of glass paints are for various surfaces. Shop your local craft stores and carefully read the labels on the paints to decide which type will work best for the job you want to do. Now you can decorate glass, tile, terracotta, porcelain, and china.

You will find that you can complete a simple project in just a few minutes. Glass painting is an enjoyable hobby that anyone can easily learn to do. Just a few basic techniques and you will be absolutely amazed at what you can create. Just remember, you can never accomplish anything until you begin. So with the help of *Glass Painting for the first time*, pick up a few paintbrushes and paints and let's begin. As we travel through each section, I will be teaching you all you need to know to create delightful and useful projects. Again, welcome to the wonderful world of glass painting!

How to Use this Book

For the person who is glass painting for the first time, this book provides a comprehensive guide to supplies, tools, and techniques that can be used to create fabulous decorative and functional objects.

Section 1: Glass Painting Basics familiarizes you with the basic tools and supplies you need to begin. Section 2: Techniques contains instructions for thirteen projects that can be made using basic glass-painting techniques. Each technique builds on that which was learned in the previous technique. From applying paint to completely cover a glass surface, to making a reverse image with a rubber stamp, to applying decorative paint strokes in a particular design. If you decide to jump ahead out of sequence, you may find you have skipped a technique you now need to use.

Section 3: Projects Beyond the Basics expands on the techniques learned in Section 2 with twelve additional projects that are a bit more complex and sometimes combine two or more techniques, such as a Dragonfly Carafe, which combines the millefiori technique that uses smooth transparent glass paints with the stained-glass technique that uses textured gel paints.

Finally, Section 4: Gallery of Artists presents designs done by artists and professionals in the field. These photographs demonstrate the fabulous effects that can be achieved through the art of glass painting and will inspire you on to creating your own masterpieces.

The intent of this book is to provide a starting point and teach basic skills. The more you practice glass painting, the more comfortable you will feel. Allow yourself a reasonable amount of time to complete your first project—remember this is your first time. You will soon discover that the techniques are easy to master.

After you have completed the first few projects, you will be surprised by how quickly you will be able to finish the remaining projects. Take pride in the talents you are developing and the unique designs only you can create.

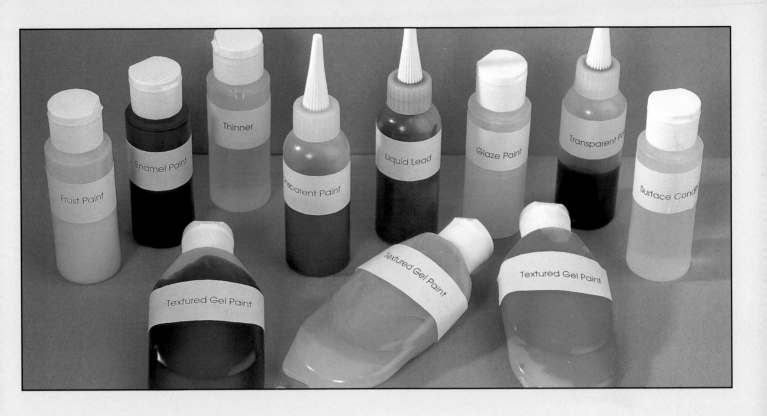

Section 1: *glass painting basics*

What do I need to get started?

If you are ready to start painting on glass, all you need to do is take a trip to the local craft store to find a wide array of glass paints and supplies. One advantage of painting on glass is that it takes very little to get started. It does not require specialized tools or equipment, just a few paintbrushes and a few bottles of paint. The rest of the equipment you need consists of items you may already have at home. Initially, you can practice on pieces you might have in your cupboard—old jelly jars, pickle jars, mismatched glasses, etc. When I first started, I used old pickle jars—I practiced everything on them. When these turn out, your time has been well spent. Paint the lid and you have a fun and inexpensive gift that can be filled with candy or bath soaps. Soon, you will find yourself opening the refrigerator—not to look for something good to eat—but for a jar that can be painted.

As you begin, give yourself time to practice and don't be too hard on yourself. Remember, practice makes perfect. Your first pieces may have an amateur look to them, but keep digging out those jelly jars. Before you know it, your skills will become more refined and you will be painting on everything you can put your hands on—and liking the results. Painting on glass is very forgiving—if you don't like what you do, simply wash it off and start again.

Here is a list of basic items you need:

Apron or cover-up for your clothes
Cotton swabs
Craft knife
Dark graphite paper, chalk-based paper, or china marker for transferring patterns
Disposable palette or foam plate
Foam stamps
Glass paints
Glassware of all sizes and shapes
Newspaper or white paper to cover work space
Paintbrushes: liner; script liner; round; shader
Paper towels
Pencil
Permanent marking pen: black
Plastic palette knife
Plastic wrap
Sponge brushes
Sponges: compressed sponge; cosmetic sponge; sea sponge
Stylus
Toothpicks
Tracing paper to copy patterns from book
Transparent tape
Water container: washtub or large low jar

You are about to start off on an addicting fun adventure that is guaranteed to bring you many hours of joy!

What will it cost to get started?

It is relatively inexpensive to get started in glass painting. The paints vary in cost from approximately $2 to $5, depending on type and brand of paint. Of course, you determine how many or few colors you would like to start with. Some of the companies have paintpot starter kits with everything you need to be able to paint available in one kit. They include the paints, surface conditioner, and finishes. These kits run approximately $4 each.

Half the fun of starting a new craft is to shop around and see what you can find that excites you and what is available on the market.

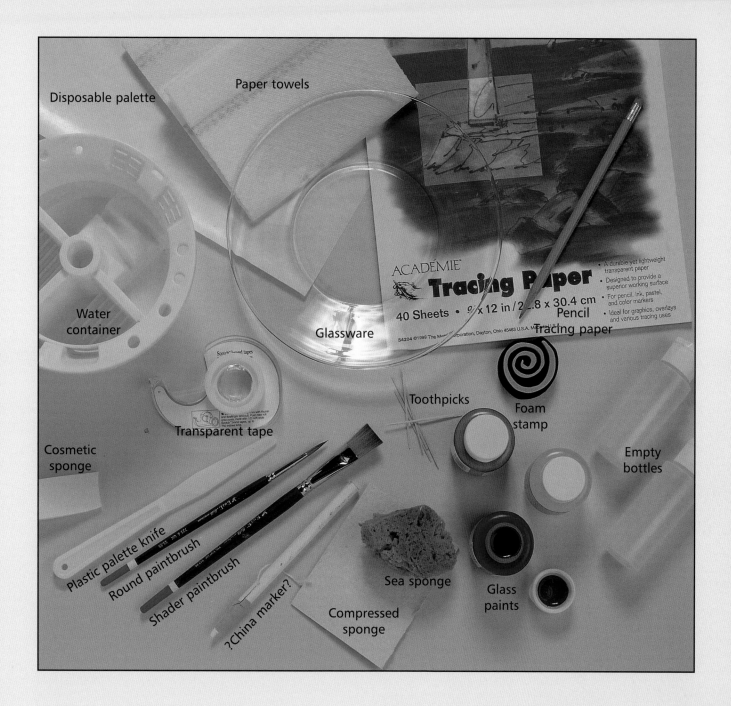

Disposable palette

Paper towels

Water container

Glassware

ACADÉMIE™
Tracing Paper
40 Sheets • 9 x 12 in / 2..8 x 30.4 cm
54204 ©1999 The Mead Corporation, Dayton, Ohio 45463 U.S.A. Made in U.S.A.

Pencil

• A durable yet lightweight transparent paper
• Designed to provide a superior working surface
• For pencil, ink, pastel, and color markers
• Ideal for graphics, overlays and various tracing uses

Tracing paper

Scotch brand tapes

Transparent tape

Toothpicks

Foam stamp

Cosmetic sponge

Empty bottles

Plastic palette knife

Round paintbrush

Shader paintbrush

?China marker?

Sea sponge

Compressed sponge

Glass paints

Paintbrushes will cost a bit, but you may already have some paintbrushes on hand that you can use. You will need a synthetic-bristled paintbrush. These range from $2 to $15 depending on the particular paintbrush and size you decide to buy. There are starter sets available on the market for approximately $11 that have almost everything in them you will need. Again, go shopping and have fun deciding on which paintbrushes you want to use for your exciting new adventure.

What types of surfaces can I paint on?

There are more surfaces available for this craft than any other. You can paint on any glass, pottery, tile, porcelain, or terra-cotta surface. Wherever you look, you will find something you want to paint on. And the delightful part about glass painting is that almost everything you paint is serviceable and useful. You don't have to worry about that question, "But what do I do with it?"

From the simplest jelly jar to the fanciest pedestal cake platter, there are no limits. Start looking around your house and you will be amazed at all the things that take on a completely different look, now that you can paint on glass. As you perfect your art and your abilities, you can think even bigger, such as mirrors and shower doors.

Have you been wanting a good excuse to go to a local flea market or garage sale? Well now is your opportunity. These are perfect places to pick up reasonably priced and sometimes quite inexpensive glass pieces in all sizes and shapes. There are beautiful old glassware pieces available if you will just shop around. If you can't find several pieces that match, don't worry. Simply paint them all with the same colors and motifs and you will have an instant "set." You can paint on fishbowls, terra-cotta pots, teapots, pitchers, and all sizes and shapes of vases.

You will be looking at glassware in a whole new light now, and you will be amazed at what you see.

What applicators do I use?

Paintbrushes
There are all types of good paintbrushes on the market to use. You may already have a few at home.

You will want a good-quality synthetic paintbrush to use with glass paints. A good synthetic paintbrush is very resilient and durable and will snap right back into shape after it has been in water. They clean out easily and will not get soft and limp after working in water and water-based paints for an extended period of time.

Avoid using a "bristle" paintbrush. These usually have long handles and are extremely stiff. They have been designed to work on canvas and to scrub paint into the surface. They are too stiff and coarse for glass painting and will leave streaks on the glass.

An expensive sable paintbrush is far too soft for painting on glass. It will absorb too much water and become limp and unmanageable after working for awhile in water and water-based products.

Paintbrush Sizes
The following sizes are recommended for painting the necessary strokes on glass:

Liner paintbrush: #1
Script liner paintbrush: #1
Shader paintbrushes: #6, #8, #10, #12
Round paintbrushes: #3, #5
Wash paintbrush: ¾"

Caring for Paintbrushes
We all learn very quickly that the best painting is done with the best quality paintbrushes. Good paintbrushes require good brush care. To get the most out of your paintbrushes, follow these simple rules:

1. New paintbrushes come with a chemical sizing in them that should be rinsed out before placing in your paint. Rinse paintbrushes often in water—especially when changing paint colors—to avoid paint buildup.

2. Clean paintbrushes on a bar of soap. Thoroughly work soap into bristles with fingers to remove paint. There are also many good brush cleaners available on the market.

3. Rinse paintbrushes until clean. Resize paintbrushes with clean soap to retain shape.

4. Store paintbrushes so bristles will not bend or roll. Protect their shape and points. Note: A soup can full of rice or beans makes a great paintbrush holder.

5. Do not leave paintbrushes sitting in water.

Note: When you are washing out your paintbrushes, remember to blot all water from the paintbrush. Glass paints are water soluble. Although this makes water cleanup possible, you do not want excess water in your paintbrush when you are working with glass paints, as they do not mix well.

Sponges
There are three major types of sponges used for various methods of sponging. These are sea sponges, compressed sponges, and cosmetic sponges.

All three will give you wonderful results, but each looks quite different from the other and is used to produce different effects and designs.

Compressed Sponge: This sponge is manufactured into a very flat sheet about ⅛" thick, making it easy to cut various shapes from it. Once the shape is cut, it is placed in water, which causes it to expand into a much thicker sponge that is very easy to use.

Compressed sponges are also readily available at all craft stores. Although almost any shape can be cut from this sponge, you will want to stay with very simple shapes. Cookie cutters are an excellent source of simple but effective designs.

These sponges must be dampened and all excess water removed each time they are used after having dried out.

Cosmetic Sponge: Cosmetic sponges can be easily found at any drug store or cosmetic counter. They are wonderful for achieving a smooth base coat when using glass paint. The finish almost looks like it has been airbrushed on. Cosmetic sponges should not be dampened before using.

Sea Sponge: This is a natural sponge that comes from the sea and is full of natural holes. It results in a very light airy look. It is readily available at all craft stores. A sea sponge must be dampened before using.

Sponge Brushes
Technically, these are not really brushes at all. A chisel-edged foam sponge is attached to the end of a handle. Because they have a large absorbent surface, sponge brushes are good for base-coating a large work surface.

Foam Stamps
These stamps are made from a dense, pliable material that is just right for stamping on a variety of surfaces. They are easy to position and lift off a surface. Foam stamps are available individually in a variety of designs as well as coordinated collections of stamps for creating themed designs.

Cotton Swabs
Available at grocery and drug stores, cotton swabs are useful for some painting techniques and quick touchups.

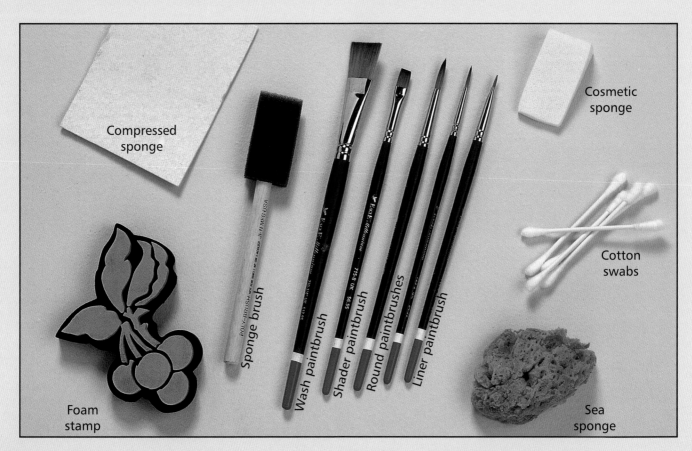

Compressed sponge

Cosmetic sponge

Cotton swabs

Foam stamp

Sponge brush

Wash paintbrush

Shader paintbrush

Round paintbrushes

Liner paintbrush

Sea sponge

How do I apply a pattern?

The simplest way to transfer a design to glass is to trace the pattern from the book onto a piece of tracing paper and tape it inside or under the glass piece.

In the case that a pattern calls for enlargement, take the book to a professional copy center. Place the pattern on the copying machine and set the enlargement as indicated on the pattern. The photocopy can then be used in the place of a traced pattern.

If you are working with a glass piece that has a curved surface, cut several slits in your pattern, enabling it to contour to the shape of the glass and result in a more accurate pattern.

If you are working on white porcelain or tile, you may want to transfer your design with dark graphite paper. There is also a chalk-based transfer paper, which simply disappears with water or as you paint.

When you are brave enough to "freehand" your designs you can use a china marker. With this tool you can sketch a pattern onto the piece and if it does not please you, you can simply wipe it off and sketch again.

What types of paints do I use?

There are many types of glass paints available on the market today. They fall into several different categories and types. There are basic glass paints, glass stains, transparent glass paints, and gel-type paints available. Each manufacturer has a wide range of colors and types of paints. Each is designed to be used in a different way. Carefully read the labels of your paints. Pay particular attention to the safety instructions on the labeling. Most glass paints are not approved to be used with food contact. Paint on the back or rim of plates, and drop down approximately ½" to leave a lip line on glasses and cups. If the piece is strictly for decorative purposes, this rule does not apply. Most of the paints are nontoxic but have not been approved for food use. Make certain to read and follow the manufacturer's instructions.

Avoid mixing different brands of glass paints. Each company formulates their particular paints with certain bases. These bases are not always compatible with each other and you will not get the best results.

Water-based Paints not Formulated for Glass: Although these acrylic paints were not formulated for glass painting, they can be used on glass. They do not need baking and are ideal for items you do not want to wash. These are well suited for use by children and for simple projects. However, they are designed for decorative purposes only and cannot be washed.

Water-based Paints Formulated for Glass: Formulated specifically for glass painting, some of these acrylics will need to be baked at 400° for 30 minutes to set. Glass pieces painted with these paints are hand-washable. These paints are easy to apply and require only soap and water cleanup.

Glass-painting Mediums: These mediums are meant to be mixed with acrylic paints for painting on glass. They vary in durability. Follow manufacturer's instructions.

Air-dry Permenamel®: This is the only air-dry, nontoxic enamel formula that does not require heat-setting. It can be used on glass, tile, terra-cotta, porcelain, pottery, mirrors, bakeware, and more. The finish is super tough, dishwasher safe (after curing 10 days), microwave safe, and oven safe (up to 350°). The full line is nontoxic and requires only water cleanup.

Surface Conditioner: Use a surface conditioner to prepare the surface for painting. This removes any dirty and oily residue on the surface and contains a bonding agent.

Retarder: If you should need to extend your paints for blending purposes, a retarder which is used to slow the drying time of these paints is also available.

Special Effects Paints: Liquid lead, transparent glass paints, and textured gel paints are also newly available. The liquid lead and transparent glass paints give you a delightful stained-glass effect. The textured gel paints allow for a three-dimensional color that can be applied to the surface with a palette knife or paintbrush. These paints enable you to obtain the many effects of hand-blown glass.

Solvent-based Paints: These paints are associated with the stained-glass industry and are not recommended for use with the designs in this book.

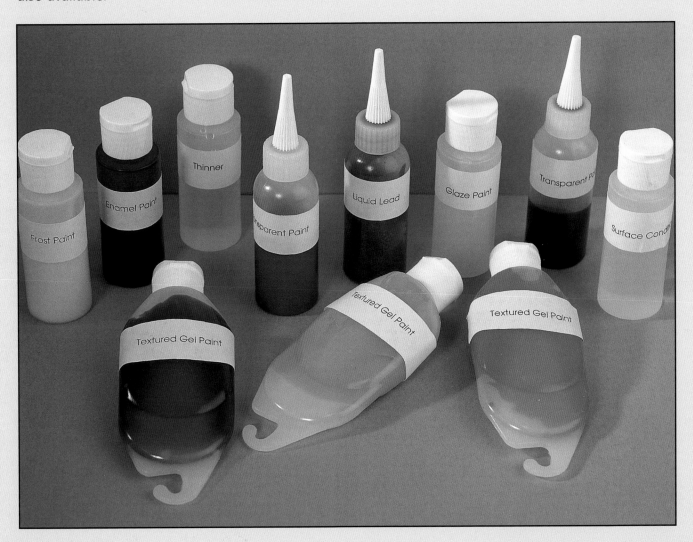

How do I complete painting on glass?

Preparing the Surface

Before painting on glass, tile, or whiteware, prepare the surface by removing any stickers. Wash surface with soap and water. Following manufacturer's instructions, apply a coat of surface conditioner to surface to be painted.

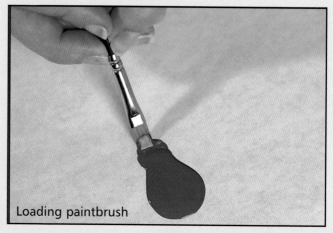
Loading paintbrush

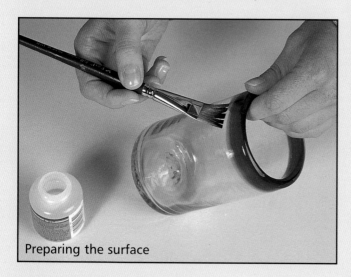
Preparing the surface

Loading Paintbrush: Hold the paintbrush at the edge of the paint puddle on the palette. Pull the paint out from the edge of the puddle toward you, loading one side of the paintbrush. Turn the paintbrush over and repeat to load the other side. Stroke the paintbrush back and forth in the paint to fully load the bristles.

Strokework Techniques

Strokework consists of properly loading your paintbrush with paint and applying pressure at the right time during the stroke while pulling the paintbrush toward you. The brush moves but does not often turn. By doing this you create the strokes used in decorative painting.

Beautiful and controlled strokework comes with practice. Practice often. When your time is limited, practice with water rather than paint in your brush.

Round Paintbrush Strokework: By using a round brush, you can paint one-strokes, s-strokes, and ribbons.

Shader Paintbrush Strokework: A flat brush has a wide (flat) side and a thin (chisel) side. The same strokes may be executed with a flat brush as with a round brush. However, the shape of the stroke will not be as rounded.

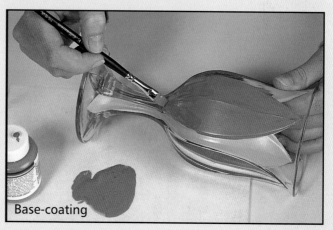
Base-coating

Base-coating: Using a loaded shader paint-brush, cover an entire area with one initial coat of paint. The paint must be smooth, without ridges or brushstrokes.

Start in the center of the project and paint out to the edges to prevent ridges on the edges. Additional coats of paint may be required for opaque coverage.

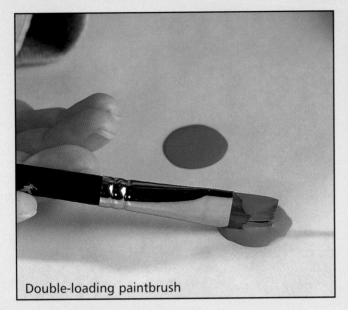

Double-loading paintbrush

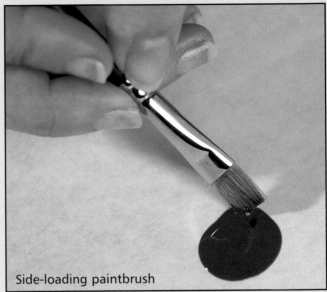

Side-loading paintbrush

Double-loading Paintbrush: Touch one edge of the shader paintbrush in the first paint color. Touch the opposite edge of the paintbrush in the second paint color.

Side-loading Paintbrush: Dampen the shader paintbrush with water and blot on a paper towel. Touch one edge of the paintbrush in the paint color. Lift paintbrush.

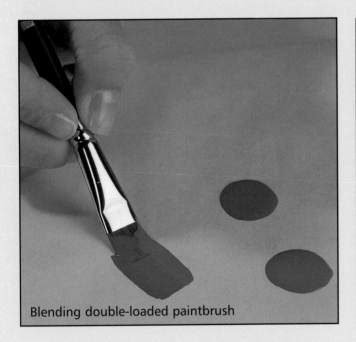

Blending double-loaded paintbrush

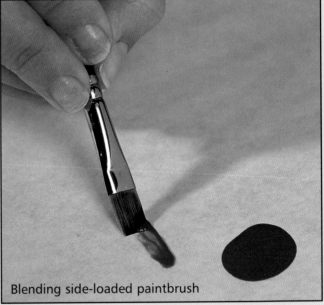

Blending side-loaded paintbrush

Blending Double-loaded Paintbrush: Stroke the double-loaded paintbrush on the palette to blend colors at the center of the paintbrush. Colors should remain unblended on the edges.

Blending Side-loaded Paintbrush: Stroke the side-loaded paintbrush on the palette until the color is full strength on one edge of the brush and dissipates into nothing at the opposite edge.

Floating shading and highlights

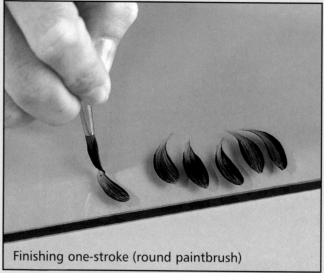

Finishing one-stroke (round paintbrush)

Floating Shading and Highlights: Side-loading is used for shading and highlights and is also called floating. Shade by side-loading with a darker color than the base color. Highlight by side-loading with a lighter color.

Finishing One-stroke (round paintbrush): As you pull, set the brush to the left or the right and start to lift the brush. The bristles will return to a point and form the tail of the stroke. As you practice, think, "PRESS...PULL...LIFT." Note: The direction you set the brush and the amount of pressure on the brush will determine size of the stroke.

Beginning one-stroke (round paintbrush)

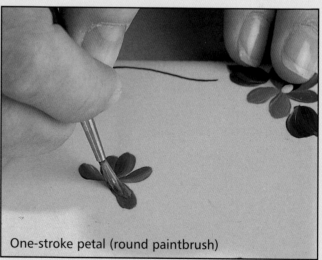

One-stroke petal (round paintbrush)

Beginning One-stroke (round paintbrush): Place the loaded round paintbrush on the glass surface. Apply pressure so the bristles spread out into a fan shape. Slowly pull the brush toward you.

One-stroke Petal (round paintbrush): Place the tip of the loaded round paintbrush on the glass surface. Press, pull, and lift the petal from the outside to the center of the flower. Note: Rotate the glass piece so you are always pulling the stroke toward you.

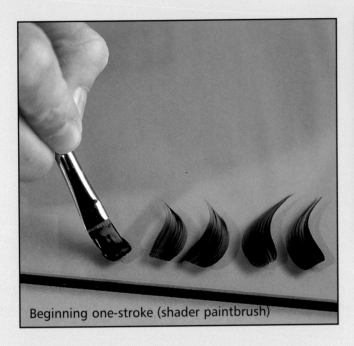

Beginning one-stroke (shader paintbrush)

Beginning One-stroke (shader paintbrush):
Place the loaded shader paintbrush on the glass surface. PRESS on the flat side and then PULL toward you.

One-stroke petal (shader paintbrush)

One-stroke Petal (shader paintbrush): For a square stroke, place the tip of the loaded shader brush on the glass surface. Apply pressure, pull, and lift the brush to a point in the center of the flower.

For a rounded stroke, immediately apply pressure, pull, and lift to finish at the center of the flower.

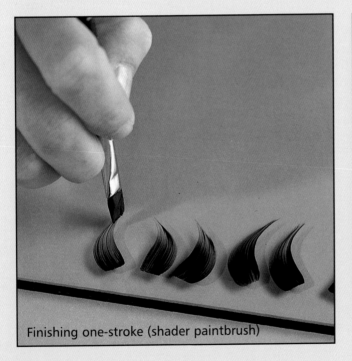

Finishing one-stroke (shader paintbrush)

Finishing One-stroke (shader paintbrush):
LIFT the brush and slide to the chisel side. Note: By applying pressure on the brush you can achieve many variations.

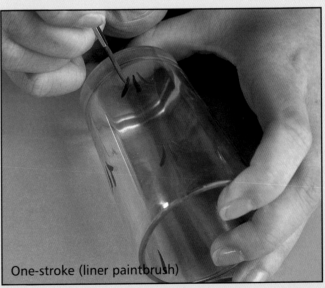

One-stroke (liner paintbrush)

One-stroke (liner paintbrush): Place the loaded liner paintbrush on the glass surface. Apply pressure so the bristles spread out into a fan shape. Slowly pull the brush toward you. As you pull, slide the brush to the left or the right and start to lift the brush. The bristles will return to a point and form the tail of the stroke.

Stroke leaf (shader paintbrush)

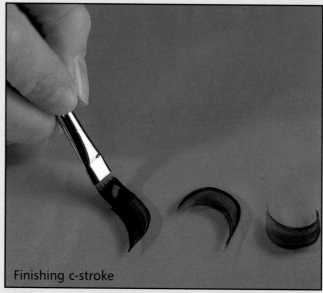

Finishing c-stroke

Stroke Leaf (shader paintbrush): Place the tip of the shader paintbrush on the glass surface, immediately applying pressure for a rounded leaf base. Pull the brush and lift to finish the stroke and create the tip of the leaf.

Finishing C-stroke: Apply pressure to lay down the paintbrush while pulling for the rounded part of the stroke. Finish the stroke by lifting the brush back up on its tip.

Beginning c-stroke

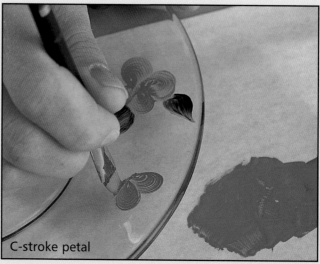

C-stroke petal

Beginning C-stroke: Holding the shader paint-brush straight up, set the tip of the brush on the glass surface. Begin pulling in the direction of the stroke as if writing the letter "C", keeping the brush on its tip.

C-stroke Petal: Holding the shader paintbrush straight up, set the tip of the brush on the glass surface with one edge at the point of the petal. Begin pulling clockwise around the of the petal, keeping the brush on its tip. Apply pressure to round off the petal and pull the brush back to the point of the petal, lifting the brush back up on its tip to finish the stroke. Note: The brush does not turn.

Combined stroke leaf (round paintbrush)

Finishing s-stroke

Combined Stroke Leaf (round paintbrush): Place the tip of the loaded round paintbrush on the glass surface and paint a one-stroke for the upper side of the leaf. Paint a small c-stroke opposite inside of the one-stroke to complete the leaf.

Finishing S-stroke: Apply pressure to lay down the paintbrush while pulling for the rounded part of the stroke. Finish the stroke by lifting the brush back up on its tip.

Beginning s-stroke

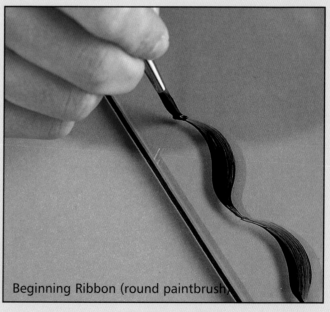

Beginning Ribbon (round paintbrush)

Beginning S-stroke: Holding the shader paintbrush straight up, set the tip of the brush on the glass surface. Begin pulling in the direction of the stroke as if writing the letter "S", keeping the brush on its tip.

Beginning Ribbon (round paintbrush): Holding the round paintbrush straight up, set the tip of the brush on the glass surface. Begin pulling to create a thin line.

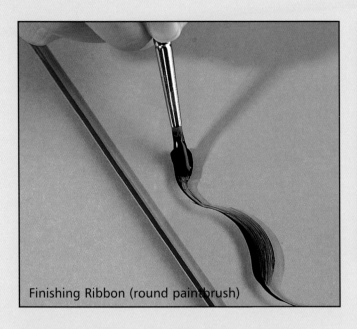

Finishing Ribbon (round paintbrush)

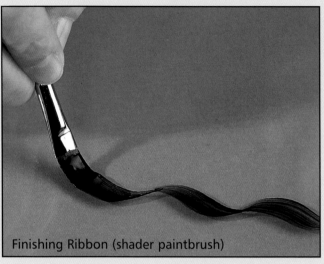

Finishing Ribbon (shader paintbrush)

Finishing Ribbon (round paintbrush): Lay down the paintbrush while pulling for the wide part of the stroke. Finish the stroke by lifting the brush back up on its tip, pulling to a fine line again. Repeat for the length of the ribbon.

Finishing Ribbon (shader paintbrush): Lay down the paintbrush while pulling for the wide part of the stroke. Finish the stroke by lifting the brush back up on its tip, pulling to a fine line again. Repeat for the length of the ribbon. Note: It is best to work this stroke from side to side, not vertically.

Beginning Ribbon (shader paintbrush)

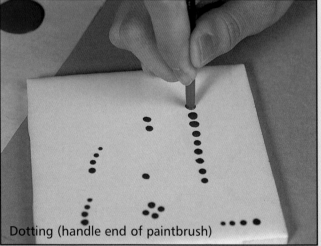

Dotting (handle end of paintbrush)

Beginning Ribbon (shader paintbrush): Holding the shader paintbrush straight up, set the tip of the brush on the glass surface. Begin pulling to create a thin line.

Dotting: For larger dots, use the handle end of a paintbrush. To make tiny dots, use the smaller end of a stylus. Dip the tool of choice in paint.

Holding the tool of choice straight up, touch it to the glass surface. For uniform dots, reload for every dot. For various sized dots, make as many dots as desired before reloading paint.

Laydowns

Laydowns: Tap the tip of the heavily loaded liner brush on the glass surface to create an oval.

Scrolls (liner paintbrush)

Scrolls (liner paintbrush): Following manufacturer's instructions, thin the paint to an inky consistency. Load the liner or script liner paintbrush with paint. Pull the brush away from the

paint puddle and roll the brush slightly to make a nice point. Note: There can be a lot of paint in the brush but not on the tip.

Holding the loaded paintbrush straight up, pull lines on flowers from the center of the petal out. Vein leaves from the stem toward the tip. Scrolls and tendrils are easier to do if you pull the brush toward you. Balance your hand on the little finger and forearm, not just fingers.

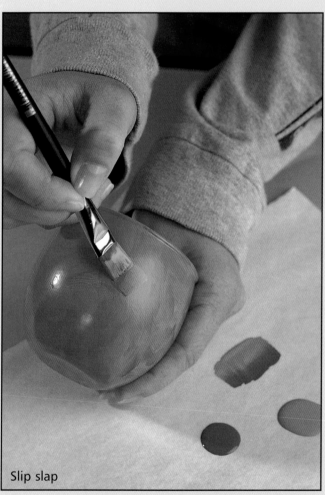
Slip slap

Slip slap: Blend two or more colors together with a crisscross brush motion. This technique works best when using the largest shader paintbrush possible for the area to be painted. Avoid over-blending the colors.

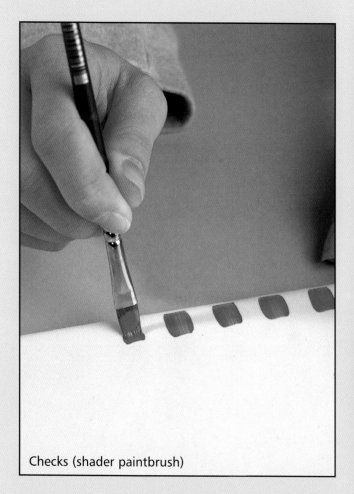

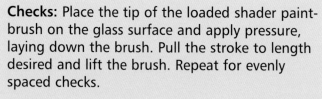

Checks (shader paintbrush)

Stipple (stipple paintbrush)

Checks: Place the tip of the loaded shader paintbrush on the glass surface and apply pressure, laying down the brush. Pull the stroke to length desired and lift the brush. Repeat for evenly spaced checks.

Stipple: Pick up paint in the tips of the bristles of a stencil brush. Tap bristles up and down on the palette to remove excess paint and to work the paint into the brush. Then tap the brush as desired on the glass surface.

Section 2: *techniques*

1
technique

What You Need to Get Started:

Foam plates
Glass vase
Paper towels
Surface conditioner
Transparent glass
   paints: kelly
   green; purple;
   red

How do I achieve a "drip and glaze" effect with glass paints?

This is the easiest technique possible for using glass paints. All you need is three coordinating shades of paint, paper towels, and a foam plate. It yields a wonderful free-form design in a very small amount of time. Try using this fabulous technique to decorate clear bulb ornaments for the holidays.

Drip & Glaze Vase

Here's How:
1. Refer to Preparing the Surface on page 19. Apply a coat of surface conditioner to inside of vase.

2. Drip red into vase.

3. Turn vase upside down on foam plate covered with paper towel, allowing color to run and drain out onto paper towel. Allow to dry. Notes: For better coverage, turn vase upside down and then right side up. Move it around on the paper towel often so it does not sit in a puddle of paint.

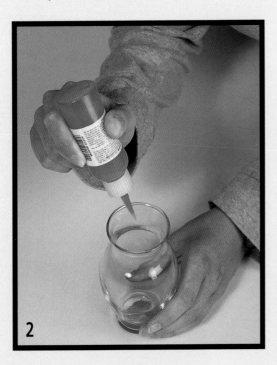

4. Repeat Steps 2–3 with purple.

5. Repeat Steps 2–3 with green.

Design Tips:

Choose only 2–3 colors as any more will muddy.

Dampen paper towel slightly to help absorb the paint that runs out of the vase and to keep paper towel from sticking to the edge of the vase.

To hurry up drying time for the vase, place it in an oven that has been preheated to 125° until it is dry. When dry, continue with the next color.

4

What You Need to Get Started:

Glass bottle or
  container with
  flat sides
Plastic wrap
Surface conditioner
Transparent glass
  paints: kelly
  green; yellow

How do I achieve a marble effect with glass paints?

This is another quick-and-easy technique that you will master in minutes. Simply apply two complementary colors to the glass piece—one after the other. The secret to the marble effect lies in knowing how to use a bit of plastic wrap. Voila! You have a stunning piece that looks as if it may have been done by Monet himself.

Marbled Bottle

Here's How:

1. Refer to Preparing the Surface on page 19. Apply a coat of surface conditioner onto glass.

2. Apply a coat of yellow directly from bottle onto the surface of one side.

3. Immediately lay a piece of plastic wrap over painted surface, squishing it around. Lift off plastic wrap. Note: This provides a base for the next color.

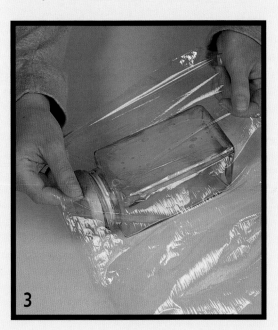

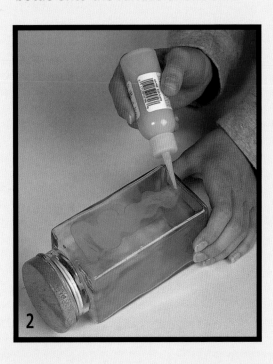

4. Randomly apply kelly green over yellow.

5. Repeat Step 3 for a marbled effect. Allow to dry flat.

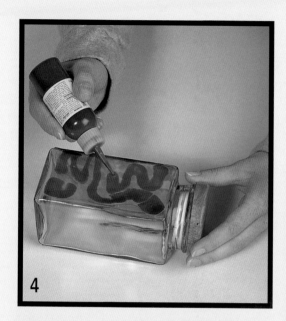

4

5

6. Repeat Steps 2–5 for each side.

Design Tips:

If the piece of glass will not lie flat, you can nestle it in a container of bird-seed or rice to hold it flat while you work and while it dries.

This technique must be worked on a flat surface, as the paint will run off of a curved surface before it is dry.

3
technique

What You Need to Get Started:

Glass bottle or container with flat sides
Surface conditioner
Toothpicks
Transparent glass paints: royal blue; kelly green; red; yellow

How do I create a millefiori design with glass paint?

Millefiori is the famous Italian technique for lampworked glass beads. The glass artist touches a rod of glass containing a flower pattern to a molten bead, leaving a small part of the rod attached to the new bead. This project mimics that concept.

Italian Glass Bottle

Here's How:

1. Refer to Preparing the Surface on page 19. Apply a coat of surface conditioner onto glass.

2. Refer to Technique 2 Steps 2–3 on page 32. Apply yellow onto surface of one side.

3. Immediately apply "drops" of royal blue, kelly green, and red onto yellow inside and on top of each other. Note: Use only 4–6 drops per millefiori design as any more will cause colors to muddy.

4. Pull a toothpick through the center of each design, cutting it into four sections. Allow to dry flat. Note: The designs will take on various shapes as they move while drying. They will not stay in the shape you first create.

5. Repeat Steps 2–4 for each side.

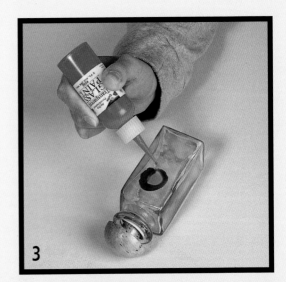

Design Tips:

To hurry up drying time for each side of the bottle, place it in an oven that has been preheated to 125° until it is dry. When dry go ahead to the next side.

If you don't like the design, simply put it in the sink before it has a chance to dry thoroughly, wash it off, and start again.

**What You Need
to Get Started:**

Compressed sponge
Craft scissors
Disposable palette
  or foam plate
Glass cup and
  pitcher
Glaze paint: clear
  gloss
Paper towel
Pencil
Permenamel paints:
  navy blue; 14K
  gold
Shader paintbrush:
  #8
Surface conditioner

How do I use a sponge
with glass paint?

It is fun and easy to apply glass paint with a sponge. Cut out any shape you can imagine from a thin compressed sponge. Place the shape in water and watch it immediately expand. There are also several preformed sponge shapes available on the market that can be used with glass paints. The simpler the shape, the better.

Sponged Stars

Here's How:
1. Draw star shapes onto sponge. Cut stars from sponge.

2. Place stars in water and allow to puff up. Blot water from sponges onto paper towel so sponges are merely damp. Set aside.

3. Refer to Preparing the Surface on page 19. Apply a coat of surface conditioner onto each piece.

4. Pour a small amount of navy blue on palette. Dip one side of star into paint and blot 3–4 times on another part of palette until sponge is evenly loaded with paint. Repeat if more paint is needed. Note: When sponge is completely loaded, carefully start applying the design.

5. Press stars onto glass surface. Allow to dry. Rinse sponge with clean water and blot dry. Note: There is no pattern necessary for the placement of this design. The stars are randomly placed depending on the surface and on how many or how few you wish to use.

6. Repeat Steps 4–5 with 14K gold, pressing stars half on and half off previously applied blue stars. Allow to dry.

7. Using shader paintbrush, carefully apply two coats of glaze over stars. Allow to dry between coats.

8. Allow paint to cure for 7–10 days before washing.

Troubleshooting:

Avoid using too much paint to prevent paint from squishing out from under the sponge while you are pressing the images.

Apply more paint to the sponge if you have spaces in the design that are not covered with paint.

Design Tips:

Save the sponge shapes. Although they will dry out, you can wet and use them again for future designs.

Use a paintbrush to daub a little color into any part of the design that doesn't get covered with paint rather than trying to restamp it.

If you need to remove part of the design, simply dampen a paper towel with surface conditioner and wipe off the design. The surface has been reconditioned and you are ready to paint.

How do I use foam stamps with glass paint?

What You Need to Get Started:

Cosmetic sponges
Foam stamps:
  checkerboard;
  cherry cluster
Glass canister
Glaze paint: clear
  gloss
Permenamel
  paints: navy blue;
  green; red
Shader paintbrush:
  #8
Surface conditioner

Foam-mounted stamps consist of an image impressed in reverse on foam rubber. They are usually bold-faced and result in a clean impression on the glass surface.

Cherry Stamped Canister

Here's How:
Note: Choose a stamp that is proportionate to the surface you are working on.

1. Refer to Preparing the Surface on page 19. Apply a coat of surface conditioner onto glass.

2. Pour a small amount of red on palette. Dip a sponge into paint and blot 3–4 times on another part of palette until sponge is evenly loaded with paint. Repeat if more paint is needed. Using sponge, load cherry section of cherry cluster stamp.

3. Pour a small amount of green on palette. Dip another sponge into paint and blot 3–4 times on another part of palette until sponge is evenly loaded with paint. Repeat if more paint is needed. Using sponge, load leaf and stem section of cherry cluster stamp.

4. Carefully stamp design onto one side of canister. Allow to dry.

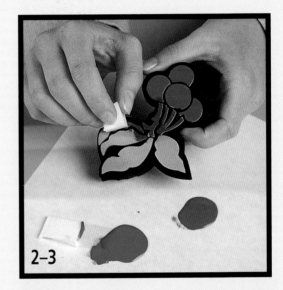

5. Repeat Steps 2–4 for each side.

6. Repeat Steps 2 and 4 with navy blue and checkerboard stamp around bottom of canister.

7. Using shader paintbrush, carefully apply two coats of glaze over painted area. Allow to dry between coats.

8. Allow paint to cure for 10 days before washing.

Troubleshooting:

When stamping on glass it is best to use a piece of cosmetic sponge or a sponge brush to load the stamp with a small amount of paint. Because you are working on a very hard, slick surface, too much paint will squish out from the edges of the stamped image or cause you to "slip" when stamping the design.

Design Tips:

Large simple images work best for stamping on glass.

There are a multitude of decorative stamps available. You can find a design that is appropriate for anyone, anyplace, or anytime.

Flat surfaces work best when stamping on glass. You can stamp on a curved surface if desired, but take time to practice rolling the stamp around the hard, slick surface.

How do I achieve reverse imaging using rubber stamps?

What You Need to Get Started:

Decorative stamp:
  swirl
Disposable palette
  or foam plate
Glass votive
  candleholder
Paper towels
Plastic palette knife
Surface conditioner
Textured gel glass
  paints: royal
  blue; purple

Reverse imaging means you are leaving a void where the design is. You are actually lifting the paint out with the rubber stamp rather than applying it.

Reverse Image Candleholder

Here's How:

1. Refer to Preparing the Surface on page 19. Apply a coat of surface conditioner onto glass.

2. Pour a small amount of paint colors on palette.

3. Using palette knife, apply purple onto top half of one side of candleholder. Note: Apply paint as you would spread butter on a slice of bread.

4. Clean palette knife on paper towel and apply blue onto bottom half of one side of candleholder.

5. Working quickly while paint is still wet, press stamp down to glass and carefully lift straight up. Allow to dry flat.

6. Clean stamp on paper towel. Repeat Steps 3–5 for each side of candleholder.

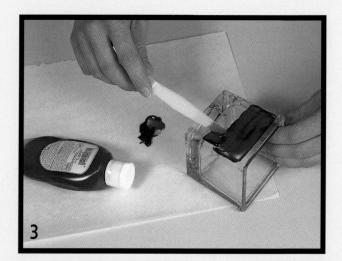

7. Allow paint to cure for 10 days before washing. Note: This paint is durable to a temperature of 350°, so burning a candle in it will not hurt the painted piece.

Troubleshooting:

For a clear and clean design, make certain to press firmly on the stamp.

Choose a stamp that is deeply cut. Regular wooden-handled rubber stamps are not cut deep enough for this technique.

Design Tip:

If there is a small area that didn't lift to the liking, you can use a cotton swab or a paintbrush to carefully lift the paint out of the design.

How do I stencil with glass paint?

Any small stencil can be used for this technique. The monogram letters were chosen because their self-adhesive backing makes them easy to use and their size is perfect for the boxes.

What You Need to Get Started:

Cosmetic sponge
Disposable palette or foam plate
Glass box
Self-adhesive stencil: letter of choice
Surface conditioner
Textured gel glass paint: royal blue

Monogrammed Box

Here's How:
1. Refer to Preparing the Surface on page 19. Apply a coat of surface conditioner onto glass.

2. Remove backing from stencil and position on box, making certain all edges are firmly adhered.

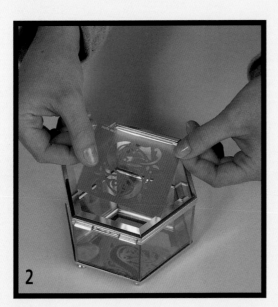

3. Tear off a small piece of cosmetic sponge. Pour a small amount of royal blue on palette. Dip sponge into paint and blot 3–4 times on another part of palette until sponge is evenly loaded with paint. Repeat if more paint is needed.

4. Sponge an even coat of royal blue onto glass within openings of stencil. Allow to dry and repeat for second coat.

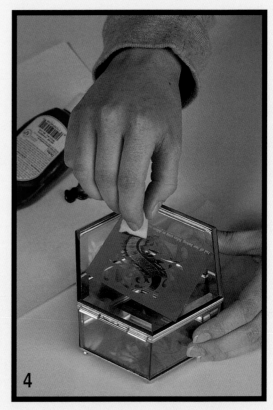

5. Carefully remove stencil.

6. Allow to dry.

Troubleshooting:
Avoid using too much paint to prevent paint from seeping under the edge of the stencil.

Avoid allowing the paint to dry too much before removing the stencil to prevent paint from peeling off when you remove the stencil. The stencil should be removed as soon as possible after the second coat of paint has been applied.

Design Tips:

These stencils require water cleanup. As soon as you finish using the stencils, thoroughly wash them with soap and water. Set aside to dry. When dry, place the sticky side down on a piece of waxed paper to store. Simply remove the waxed paper the next time you need to use them.

Any small stencil design can be used for these boxes. If the stencil doesn't have a sticky back, spray it with a repositionable adhesive, following the manufacturer's instructions.

You can use this technique to make beautiful glass Christmas ornaments, personalized glasses or goblets, or to personalize any glass piece you might have. Even a jelly jar with a fancy initial on it, filled with homemade jelly and tied with a big bow, would make a perfect gift.

8
technique

**What You Need
to Get Started:**

Cosmetic sponges
Glass dessert
  dishes
Glaze paint: clear
  gloss
Permenamel
  paints: bright
  green; lavender;
  peach; red
Shader paintbrush:
  #8
Surface conditioner
Transparent tape

How do I achieve
stenciling effects with tape?

There is no right or wrong way to create the design for this particular technique. Any way you can apply tape to glass will result in an interesting and unique design. Because the tape is expendable, you do not have to worry about keeping your supplies free of errant paint. Simply throw used tape away when you are finished painting the design!

Geometric Dessert Dishes

Here's How:

1. Refer to Preparing the Surface on page 19. Apply a coat of surface conditioner onto each piece.

2. Apply tape to create evenly spaced stripes and shapes.

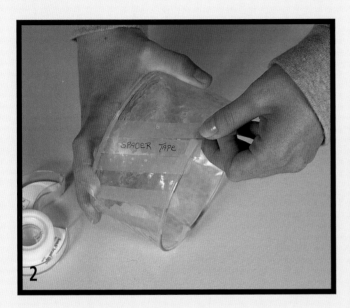

3. Pour paints onto palette. Using a separate cosmetic sponge for each paint color, base-coat each color as desired. Allow to dry and repeat for second coat. Remove tape immediately after applying last coat.

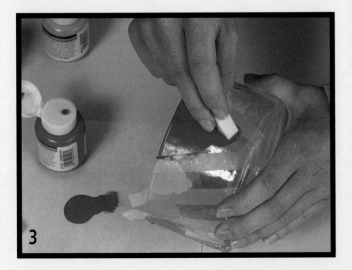

4. Using shader paintbrush, carefully apply two coats of glaze over paint. Allow to dry between coats.

Troubleshooting:

Good tape adhesion will make for a sharp line on the finished piece. Make certain to go along each edge of the tape with your finger or a pencil eraser, pressing it firmly to the glass to prevent paint from seeping under the tape.

Design Tip:

Use various sizes of tape to achieve different effects.

How do I achieve a stained-glass look with transparent glass paint?

Empty paint
 bottles (7)
Glass vase: square
Glaze paint: clear
 gloss
Liquid lead
Pencil
Surface conditioner
Tracing paper
Transparent glass
 paints: amber;
 blue; kelly green;
 red; rose; white;
 yellow
Transparent tape

A relatively new type of glass paint is available that creates the appearance of stained-glass leading. Once you draw the outline of the pattern on the glass piece, simply fill in between the lines with the different colors of paint. This technique is a lot like coloring a picture in a coloring book.

Oriental Vase

Here's How:

1. Refer to Preparing the Surface on page 19. Apply a coat of surface conditioner onto glass.

2. Trace Fish Pattern and Leaf Pattern on page 48 onto tracing paper and tape them inside vase.

3. Applying liquid lead directly from the bottle, trace over lines of pattern to lead entire design on one side of vase. Allow to dry.

4. Mix the following colors in empty paint bottles, using one bottle per mixture:
Green – 4 parts green, 3 parts
 glaze, 1 part amber
Yellow – 4 parts yellow, 2
 parts amber
Orange – 4 parts yellow, 3
 parts red, 1 part amber

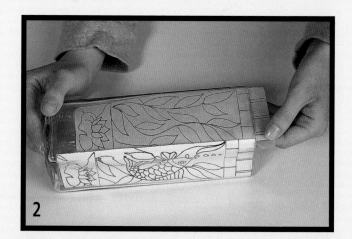

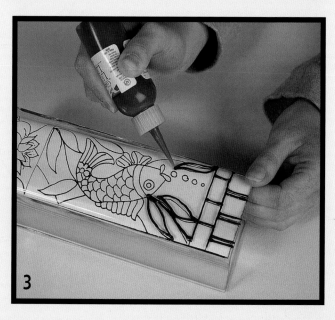

Rose – 4 parts rose, 1 part amber
Amber – 4 parts amber, 4 parts glaze
Medium Blue – 4 parts white, 2 parts blue, 1 part amber, 1 part glaze
Light Blue – 3 parts Medium Blue mixture, 3 parts white

5. Apply one color at a time directly from the bottle and into place on one leaded side of vase as follows:
Leaves – Green mixture and Amber mixture
Fish – Green mixture, Orange mixture, Amber mixture, and Yellow mixture
Background – Light Blue mixture
Top Band and Stripes – Medium Blue mixture and Rose mixture
Second Band – Orange mixture
Water Lily – Rose mixture
Water Lily Leaf – Green mixture
Background – Medium Blue mixture
Tear Drops – Orange mixture

Apply paint tightly against lead, making certain there are no gaps. Allow to dry.

6. Repeat Steps 3–5 for each side of vase.

Design Tips:

Try using other designs with this technique. Simple designs from a coloring book or any pattern with very simple, uncluttered lines can be used.

Experiment and try your own colors. Try painting a smaller, simpler design, such as a suncatcher, with this same technique.

Fish Pattern

Leaf Pattern

10
technique

How do I achieve a textured effect with glass paints?

This project not only has a stained-glass look, but it is made even more dimensional with the addition of textured gel glass paints. When this paint dries, it is raised and bumpy, much the same as it was when it was applied to the piece.

Textured Suncatcher

Here's How:

1. Refer to Preparing the Surface on page 19. Apply a coat of surface conditioner onto glass.

2. Enlarge Suncatcher Pattern on opposite page. Tape photocopy onto underside of suncatcher.

3. Applying liquid lead directly from the bottle, trace over lines of pattern to lead entire design. Allow to dry.

4. Pour textured gel glass paints onto palette. Using round paintbrush, scoop up one color at a time and pat it into place as follows:
Leaves – lime green
Flower petals – fill in with golden yellow and shade with orange
Centers – dots of liquid lead

Apply paint tightly against leading, making certain there are no gaps. Allow to dry.

Troubleshooting:
Avoid using too much paint or applying it on too thickly to prevent any creasing or cracking down the center of the paint when it is dry.

Design Tip:
Try using this design on a variety of pieces. It is very adaptable to any shape. You may even want to try free-handing some of these "floppy flowers" on a piece.

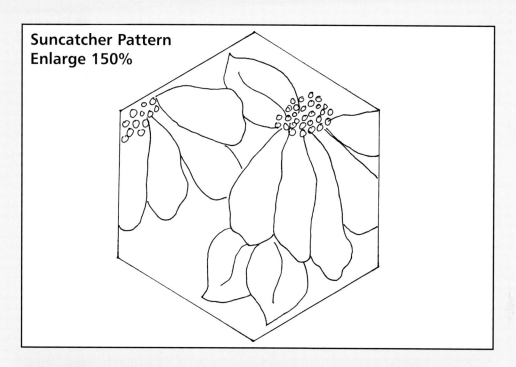

**Suncatcher Pattern
Enlarge 150%**

What You Need to Get Started:

Glass goblet with embossed design
Glaze paint: clear gloss
Permenamel paints: 14K gold; pine green; seafoam green; rose
Round paintbrush: #3
Shader paint-brushes: #8; #12
Surface conditioner

How do I paint embossed glass?

Accent a design that already exists on embossed glass by painting it. The glass provides a pattern for painting while the opaque paint gives a more solid look to the glass.

Tulip Goblet

Here's How:
Note: Refer to Strokework Techniques on pages 19–27.

1. Refer to Preparing the Surface on page 19. Apply a coat of surface conditioner onto glass.

2. Using #12 shader paintbrush, base-coat each section of embossed glass, alternating seafoam green and rose. Allow to dry and repeat for second coat.

3. Using #8 shader paintbrush double-loaded with seafoam green and pine green, paint along outer edge of seafoam green section, placing edge of paintbrush with pine green toward outside. Allow to dry.

4. Using round paintbrush loaded with gold, paint laydowns on rose-colored "petals." Allow to dry.

5. Using #12 shader paintbrush, apply two coats of clear gloss glaze over petals. Allow to dry between coats.

Design Tip:
Shop thrift stores for pieces of embossed glass. Most large discount stores also carry embossed glass.

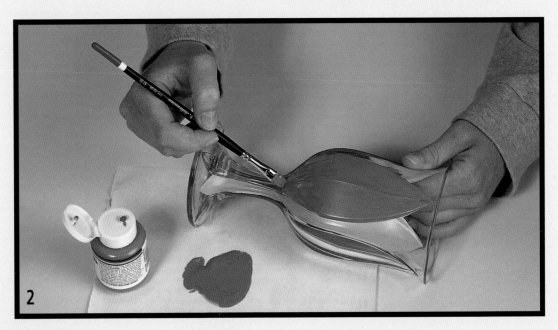

2

How do I achieve reverse glass painting?

What You Need to Get Started:

Glass plate with grape embossed pattern on the underside
Glaze paint: clear gloss
Permenamel paints: brown; bright green; green; pine green; lavender; purple; white
Permenamel thinner dilutant
Round paintbrush: #3
Shader paintbrushes: #8; #12
Surface conditioner
Wash paintbrush: ¾"

Reverse glass painting means the design is painted in a reverse order. What you see in the front of a design is what you paint first and work your way to the background.

Fruit Plate

Here's How:
Note: Refer to Strokework Techniques on pages 19–27.

1. Refer to Preparing the Surface on page 19. Apply a coat of surface conditioner onto the back side of plate.

2. Using #8 shader paintbrush side-loaded with white, float a highlight mark on each grape.

3. Float the following colors for shading and highlighting:
Shade Leaves – pine green
Shade Grapes – purple
Highlight Grapes – lavender plus white
Highlight Leaves – bright green

4. Using #12 shader paintbrush loaded with lavender, paint over grape area. Allow to dry and repeat for second coat.

2–4

5. Using #12 shader paintbrush loaded with green, paint over leaves area. Allow to dry and repeat for second coat.

6. Using round paintbrush loaded with brown, paint over stem area. Allow to dry and repeat for second coat.

7. Using wash paintbrush, evenly apply two coats of glaze over paint on back of plate. Allow to dry between coats.

Design Tip:
Choose autumn colors and paint light green grapes with golden leaves.

13
technique

What You Need to Get Started:

Frosting kit: white
Glass plate, bowl, and goblet
Shader paintbrush: #8
Surface conditioner
Tracing paper
Transparent tape

Give a cut-crystal look to ordinary glassware. When applied to glass, frosting medium creates an etched effect that is subtle yet very appealing to the eye. This white-on-white sort of color scheme goes perfectly with any home-decorating theme.

Frosted Florals

Here's How:
Note: Refer to Strokework Techniques on pages 19–27.

1. Refer to Preparing the Surface on page 19. Apply a coat of surface conditioner onto each piece.

2. Enlarge Florals Pattern on opposite page. Tape photocopy onto underside of plate and inside bowl and goblet.

3. Using shader paintbrush loaded with frosting medium, paint four c-strokes to form petals of flower.

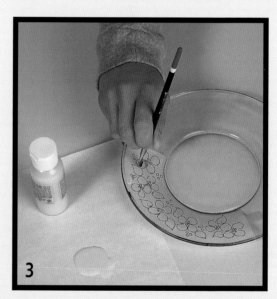

4. Using handle end of paintbrush loaded with frosting medium, paint several dots in each flower center.

5. Using shader paintbrush loaded with frosting medium, paint stroke leaves to side of each flower.

Troubleshooting:
Avoid using a glaze of any kind over this medium or it will disappear.

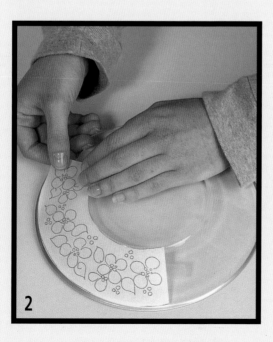

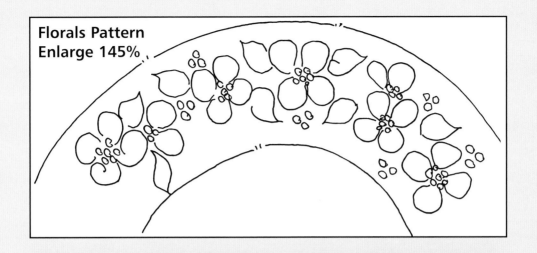

**Florals Pattern
Enlarge 145%**

Section 3: *projects beyond the basics*

1
project

What You Need to Get Started:

Compressed sponge
Craft scissors
Glaze paint: clear gloss
Lamp shade
Lamp works kit
Paper towels
Pencil
Permanent marking pen: black
Permenamel paints: goldenrod; lilac; purple; red; turquoise; white; yellow
Quart jar
Surface conditioner
Tracing paper
Wash paintbrush: ¾"

How do I combine paint colors on a sponge?

Empty that jar full of fruit and turn it into a darling lamp. This one is decorated with multicolored hearts. The same hearts are repeated on the lamp shade.

Heart to Heart Canning Jar Lamp

Here's How:
Note: Permenamel paints are not normally recommended for painting on fabric. However, I used them to paint the lamp shade so the colors would coordinate.

1. Using pencil, trace Heart Patterns on opposite page onto tracing paper. Cut out traced patterns and trace onto sponge. Cut hearts from sponge.

2. Place hearts in water and allow to puff up. Blot water from sponge onto paper towel so sponge is merely damp. Set aside.

3. Refer to Preparing the Surface on page 19. Apply a coat of surface conditioner to jar.

4. Using wash paintbrush loaded with white, base-coat jar. Allow to dry and repeat for second coat.

5. Refer to Technique 4 Steps 4–5 on pages 36–37. Load largest heart sponge with yellow and press onto jar and lamp shade.

6. Refer to Technique 4 Step 6, loading sponge with goldenrod.

7. Repeat Steps 5–6 using the following color combinations:
    purple/turquoise
    red/lilac
    lilac/purple
    yellow/purple

Allow to dry.

8. Using permanent marking pen, randomly outline a few hearts on jar and lamp shade.

9. Using wash paintbrush, evenly apply two coats of glaze over entire surface of jar. Allow to dry between coats.

10. Insert lamp works into jar.

Heart Patterns

How do I combine paint types and techniques?

Disposable palette or foam plate
Glass carafe and goblet
Liquid lead
Plastic wrap
Round paintbrush: #3
Surface conditioner
Textured gel glass paints: royal blue; pearl
Tracing paper
Transparent glass paints: royal blue; white
Transparent tape

This elegant project combines the smooth effects of transparent glass paint in the millefiori technique with textured gel paints in a stained-glass technique.

Dragonfly Carafe & Goblet

Here's How:
1. Refer to Preparing the Surface on page 19. Apply a coat of surface conditioner to carafe and goblet. Set goblet aside.

2. Refer to Technique 3 Steps 2–5 on page 34. Paint the lower portion of the carafe with royal blue and white transparent glass paints.

3. Trace Dragonfly Pattern below onto tracing paper and tape it inside upper portion of carafe.

4. Refer to Technique 9 Step 3 on page 46. Apply liquid lead.

5. Pour textured gel glass paints onto palette. Using round paintbrush, pat royal blue into dragonfly tail and dot on eyes. Mix royal blue and pearl together and pat into dragonfly body. Pat pearl and pearl/royal blue mixture into dragonfly wings. Allow to dry.

6. Repeat Steps 3–5 for goblet.

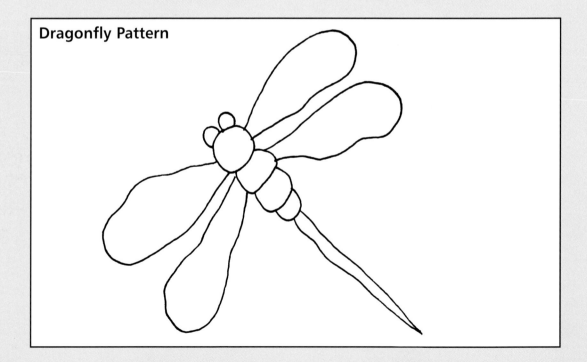

Dragonfly Pattern

3
project

What You Need to Get Started:

Cotton swabs
Disposable palette
  or foam plate
Glass candlestick,
  potpourri bowl,
  small votive
  candleholders (2)
Liner paintbrush:
  #1
Permenamel paints:
  fuchsia; hunter
  green; pink;
  white
Round paintbrush:
  #3
Shader paintbrush:
  #6
Silicone adhesive
Stylus

Create a coordinating set of candleholders by adhering two glass pieces together to form a new piece. This particular set is painted with rosettes made with the end of a cotton swab.

Pink Rosette Candleholders

Here's How:
Note: Refer to Strokework Techniques on pages 19–27.

1. Remove any stickers from glass. Wash surface with soap and water.

2. Apply a bead of silicone adhesive around top edge of candlestick. Set potpourri bowl on top of candlestick. Following manufacturer's instructions, allow to dry.

3. Turn one small votive candleholder upside down and apply a bead of silicone adhesive around edge of candleholder. Set remaining candleholder on top. Allow to dry.

4. Following manufacturer's instructions, apply a coat of surface conditioner to each piece.

5. Using shader paintbrush loaded with white, base-coat top of candlestick and underside of candlestick base. Allow to dry and repeat for second coat.

6. Pour a small amount of fuchsia and pink paints on palette. Dip half of cotton swab end into pink and half into fuchsia.

7. Place loaded cotton swab end onto potpourri bowl, give a half twist, and lift. This will automatically make a two-colored rosette.

8. Using round paintbrush loaded with hunter green, paint two laydowns on one side of rosette and one laydown on opposite side to make leaves.

9. Repeat Steps 6–8 for candlestick base and upside down small votive candleholder.

10. Repeat Steps 6–8 excluding third laydown leaf around top of candlestick and along top edge of top small votive candleholder.

11. Using stylus loaded with white, paint three dots between rosettes on potpourri bowl and upside down small votive holder.

12. Using shader paintbrush loaded with fuchsia, paint stripes around bottom edge of potpourri bowl. Allow to dry.

13. Using liner paintbrush loaded with white, paint a thin white stripe on each fuchsia stripe. Paint around top edge of potpourri bowl. Allow to dry.

14. Using round paintbrush loaded with fuchsia, paint around bottom edge of candlestick and alternating sections around middle of candlestick. Allow to dry.

15. Using shader paintbrush, evenly apply two coats of glaze over entire surface of each piece. Allow to dry between coats.

4
project

How do I coordinate different pieces of whiteware?

What You Need to Get Started:

Compressed sponge
Craft scissors
Disposable palette or foam plate
Glaze paint: clear gloss
Liner paintbrush: #1
Permenamel shimmer paints: blue; gold; green; orange; purple; raspberry
Round paintbrush: #3
Shader paintbrushes: #4; #6; #8; #10
Surface conditioner
Wash paintbrush: ¾"
Whiteware cup, saucer, sugar bowl, teapot

Make ordinary dishes extraordinary by painting each piece with variations of the same motifs. This tea set is painted with shimmer paints in a combination of dots, ribbons, and stripes.

Funky Tea Set

Here's How:
Note: Refer to Strokework Techniques on pages 19–27.

1. Refer to Preparing the Surface on page 19. Apply a coat of surface conditioner onto each piece.

2. Cut ⅜" square from sponge.

3. Place square in water and allow to puff up. Blot water from sponge onto paper towel so sponge is merely damp.

4. Refer to Technique 4 Step 4 on page 36. Load square sponge with purple.

5. Press evenly spaced squares onto bottom edge of teapot and cup and allow to dry. Rinse sponge with clean water and blot dry.

6. Using #8 shader paintbrush loaded with blue, paint spout, handle, band on lid, and vertical stripe on teapot. Paint stripes on cup and bowl.

7. Using #10 shader paintbrush loaded with gold, paint large ribbon line, knob on lid, and band around top of teapot.

8. Using #4 shader paintbrush loaded with orange, paint medium ribbon line on teapot.

9. Using #8 shader paintbrush loaded with gold, paint large ribbon line on cup and bowl.

10. Using #6 shader paintbrush loaded with gold, paint thick lines for plaid in center of plate.

11. Using round paintbrush loaded with orange, paint thin lines for plaid in center of plate. Paint small ribbon lines on teapot, bowl, and cup.

12. Using round paintbrush loaded with raspberry, paint ribbon line in center of plate.

13. Using round paintbrush loaded with blue, paint large scallop line on plate. Paint ribbon line on bowl.

14. Using round paintbrush loaded with purple, paint laydowns on plate.

15. Using handle end of paintbrush loaded with raspberry, paint four dots for petals of flowers on lid, teapot, plate, and cup.

16. Using handle end of paintbrush loaded with gold, paint dots for centers of flowers on lid, teapot, plate, and cup.

17. Using liner paintbrush loaded with green, paint one-stroke stems and leaves on lid, teapot, plate, and cup. Paint thin line on bowl.

18. Using liner paintbrush loaded with raspberry, paint ribbon lines around top and bottom of design on cup.

19. Using wash paintbrush, evenly apply two coats of glaze over entire surface of each piece. Allow to dry between coats.

Design Tip:
    Change the colors and use this same design on clay pots for your patio or garden. Fill the pots with flowering plants.

How do I combine sponging with paint strokes?

What You Need to Get Started:

Compressed
  sponge
Craft scissors
Dark graphite
  paper
Disposable palette
  or foam plate
Glass candlestick,
  potpourri bowl,
  small votive
  candleholders
  (2), stackable
  votive candle-
  holders (2)
Glaze paint: clear
  gloss
Liner paintbrush:
  #1
Paper towels
Pencil
Permanent mark-
  ing pen: black
Permenamel
  paints: black;
  green; orange;
  red iron oxide;
  tangerine; white
Ribbon of choice
Round paintbrush:
  #3
Shader paintbrush:
  #10
Silicone adhesive
Stencil paint-
  brushes: ¼"; 1"
Stylus
Surface conditioner
Tracing paper
Wash paintbrush:
  ¾"

These Halloween candleholders are just right for setting the mood for a spooky holiday. Three jack-o'-lantern faces light up on an orange background as a cheeky ghost says "boo." Copy the provided patterns for sponge shapes and simple paint strokes and you will be done in no time at all.

Halloween Candle Bowls
Photograph on page 71.

Here's How:
Note: Refer to Strokework Techniques on pages 19–27.

1. Remove any stickers from glass. Wash surface with soap and water.

2. Apply a bead of silicone adhesive around top edge of candlestick. Set potpourri bowl on top of candlestick. Following manufacturer's instructions, allow to dry.

3. Turn one small votive candleholder upside down and apply a bead of silicone adhesive around edge of candleholder. Set remaining small votive candleholder on top. Allow to dry.

4. Following manufacturer's instructions, apply a coat of surface conditioner to each piece.

5. Using wash paintbrush loaded with tangerine, base-coat all pieces, excluding the candlestick and upside down small votive candleholder. Allow to dry and repeat for second coat.

6. Using wash paintbrush side-loaded with orange, paint a slip-slap coat over each tangerine piece. Allow to dry.

7. Using shader paintbrush loaded with black, base-coat upside down small votive candleholder and under-side of candlestick base. Allow to dry and repeat for second coat.

8. Trace Pumpkin Face Pattern on opposite page onto tracing paper. Using dark graphite paper, transfer traced pattern onto potpourri bowl, top small votive candleholder, and bottom stacked votive candleholder.

9. Using 1" stencil paintbrush loaded with orange and then red iron oxide, stipple on pumpkins' cheeks.

10. Using round paintbrush loaded with black, paint nose and mouth.

11. Using pencil, trace Eyes Pattern, Ghost Pattern, and Leaf Pattern on opposite page onto tracing paper. Cut out traced patterns and trace onto sponge. Using scissors, cut eyes, ghost, and leaves from sponge.

(continued on page 70)

Ghost Pattern

Leaf Pattern

Boo Pattern

Eyes Pattern

Pumpkin Face Pattern

(continued from page 68)

12. Place eyes, ghost, and leaf in water and allow to puff up. Blot water from sponges onto paper towel so sponges are merely damp. Set ghost and leaf aside.

13. Refer to Technique 4 Step 4 on page 36. Load eye sponge with black.

14. Evenly press eye onto pumpkin face. Allow to dry. Rinse sponge with clean water and blot dry.

15. Using handle end of paintbrush loaded with white, paint "sparkle" dots on cheeks, eyes, and nose.

16. Refer to Technique 4 Step 4 on page 36. Load ghost sponge with white.

17. Evenly press ghost onto remaining stacked votive candleholder. Allow to dry. Rinse sponge with clean water and blot dry.

18. Using ¼" stencil paintbrush loaded with orange, stipple on ghosts' cheeks.

19. Using round paintbrush loaded with black, paint laydowns for eyes and mouth on ghost.

20. Using handle end of paintbrush loaded with white, paint "sparkle" dots on cheeks and eyes.

21. Using pencil, trace Boo Pattern on page 69 onto tracing paper. Using dark graphite paper, transfer traced pattern onto stacked votive candle holder next to ghost.

22. Using liner paintbrush loaded with black, paint "Boo" lettering.

23. Refer to Technique 4 Step 4 on page 36. Load leaf sponge with green.

24. Evenly press leaf onto each pumpkin as desired. Allow to dry. Rinse sponge with clean water and blot dry.

25. Using shader paintbrush loaded with orange, paint checks around bottom edge of potpourri bowl and top edge of stacked votive candleholder.

26. Using round paintbrush loaded with orange, paint around bottom edge of candlestick.

27. Using stylus loaded with black, randomly paint dots around upside down small votive holder and candlestick base.

28. Using round paintbrush loaded with green, base-coat alternating sections around the middle of candlestick. Allow to dry.

29. Using permanent marking pen, outline ghost, leaves, and corners of mouths on pumpkins.

30. Using wash paintbrush, evenly apply two coats of glaze over entire surface of each piece. Allow to dry between coats.

31. Tie ribbon into a bow around each piece and enjoy.

Design Tip:

Gather a bunch of glass containers and stack or combine them to make interesting arrangements. You'll be delightfully surprised at how many combinations you can come up with.

How do I use part of a design on a smaller glass surface?

This happy little snowman trivet would make a great gift for friends and neighbors. Festive mugs with matching faces make that hot cocoa taste even better.

What You Need to Get Started:

Ceramic tile: white, 6"-square
Compressed sponge
Craft scissors
Dark graphite paper
Disposable palette or foam plate
Glaze paint: clear gloss
Liner paintbrush: #1
Paper towels
Pencil
Permanent marking pen: black
Permenamel paints: black; light blue; clay; hunter green; orange; red; red iron oxide; white
Round paintbrush: #3
Shader paintbrush: #10
Stencil paintbrush: 1"
Surface conditioner
Tracing paper
Wash paintbrush: ¾"

Snowman Tile Trivet & Cocoa Mug
Photograph on page 74.

Here's How:
Note: Refer to Strokework Techniques on pages 19–27.

1. Refer to Preparing the Surface on page 19. Apply a coat of surface conditioner onto each piece.

2. Using pencil, trace Snowman Tile Pattern on opposite page onto tracing paper. Using dark graphite paper, transfer traced pattern onto front of tile.

3. Using shader paintbrush loaded with hunter green, paint hat. Using round paintbrush loaded with red, paint stripes.

4. Using stencil paintbrush loaded with red and then clay, stipple on snowman cheeks.

5. Using round paintbrush loaded with black, paint eyes and coal teeth.

6. Using round paintbrush double-loaded with orange and red iron oxide, paint carrot nose.

7. Using shader paintbrush side-loaded with light blue, float shading to the left side of the eyes and nose.

8. Using shader paintbrush side-loaded with white, float a highlight on eyes.

9. Using liner paintbrush loaded with white, paint one-strokes for "sparkles" on eyes.

10. Using stylus loaded with white, paint "sparkle" dots on eyes and cheeks.

11. Using round paintbrush loaded with red, paint bow tie, buttons, and around edge of tile.

12. Using permanent marking pen, outline carrot nose and draw in mouth and crow's feet.

13. Using wash paintbrush, evenly apply two coats of glaze over entire surface. Allow to dry between coats.

14. Repeat Steps 1–2 using Snowman Mug Pattern. Repeat Steps 4–10 to paint mugs.

15. Using shader paintbrush loaded with red, paint bottom edge of mug.

16. Using shader paintbrush loaded with hunter green, paint handle.

17. Cut ½" square from sponge.
(continued on page 74)

Snowman Tile Pattern

Snowman Mug Pattern

73

(continued from page 72)
18. Place square in water and allow to puff up. Blot water from sponge onto paper towel so sponge is merely damp.

19. Refer to Technique 4 Step 4 on page 36. Load square sponge with white.

20. Press evenly spaced squares onto handle. Allow to dry. Rinse sponge with clean water and blot dry.

21. Repeat Steps 12–13 for mugs.

How do I use one-stroke painting on whiteware?

Turn an ordinary white tile into a beautiful clock. Recycle those old teacups and saucers into beautiful candleholders.

Violet Clock & Teacup Votive Candleholder

Photograph on page 77.

Here's How:

Note: Refer to Strokework Techniques on pages 19–27. Wear safety glasses when using power tools.

1. Remove any stickers from whiteware.

2. Using ruler and permanent marking pen, mark center of tile.

3. Carefully drill hole in center of tile to accommodate clock works.

4. Wash tile and whiteware surfaces with soap and water. Following manufacturer's instructions, apply a coat of surface conditioner.

5. Using pencil, trace all patterns on page 76 onto tracing paper. Using dark graphite paper, transfer traced Saucer Violets Pattern and Cup Violets Pattern around border of saucer and cup. Using dark graphite paper, transfer traced Tile Violets Pattern onto front of tile.

6. Using round paintbrush loaded with purple and then white, paint four small one-strokes for bottom petals on each violet. Paint two slightly larger one-strokes from opposite directions into each other to form top petal.

Repeat for all violets.

7. Using round paintbrush loaded with purple, paint small laydown in the center of violet. Using round paintbrush loaded with yellow, paint smaller laydown on top. Repeat for all violets.

8. Using liner paintbrush double-loaded with green and hunter green, paint leaves with combination of an s-stroke and a c-stroke.

9. Using script liner paintbrush loaded with green and then hunter green, create scrolls and one-strokes.

10. Using round paintbrush loaded with purple and then white, paint around edge of tile.

11. Using shader paintbrush, evenly apply two coats of glaze over painted areas. Allow to dry between coats.

12. Turn teacup upside down. Apply a bead of silicone adhesive around bottom of cup. Set saucer on top of cup. Following manufacturer's instructions, allow to dry.

13. Tie ribbon into a bow on handle of teacup.

14. Place votive candle in center of saucer.

15. Following manufacturer's instructions, apply clock face and insert clock works.

What You Need to Get Started:

Ceramic tile: white, 6"-square
Clock face
Clock works kit
Dark graphite paper
Disposable palette or foam plate
Electric drill with $5/16$"-dia. masonry bit
Glaze paint: clear gloss
Liner paintbrush: #1
Permanent marking pen: black
Permenamel paints: green; hunter green; purple; white; yellow
Round paintbrush: #3
Ruler
Script liner paintbrush: #3
Shader paintbrush: #10
Silicone adhesive
Small piece of ribbon
Surface conditioner
Tracing paper
Votive candle
Whiteware cup and saucer

Saucer Violets Pattern

Cup Violets Pattern

Tile Violets Pattern

8
project

What You Need to Get Started:

Disposable palette or foam plate
Glass vase
Permenamel paints: goldenrod; green; hunter green; tangerine; white; yellow
Round paintbrush: #5
Surface conditioner
Tracing paper
Transparent tape

How do I paint a one-stroke daisy using a round paintbrush?

The majority of this design is made up of one-strokes. The round paintbrush causes the daisy petals to appear delicate and drooping. The two-toned leaves add to the overall soft look.

One-stroke Daisies Vase

Here's How:
Note: Refer to Strokework Techniques on pages 19–27.

1. Refer to Preparing the Surface on page 19. Apply a coat of surface conditioner onto glass.

2. Enlarge Daisies Vase Pattern below. Tape photocopy inside vase, wrapping the design so A's meet.

3. Using round paintbrush loaded with white, paint one-stroke daisy petals.

4. Using round paintbrush loaded with goldenrod, tap in daisy centers. While still wet, add tangerine to lower right of each center and yellow to upper left of each center. Allow to dry.

5. Using round paintbrush double-loaded with green and hunter green, paint s-stroke leaves.

6. Allow paint to cure for 10 days before using.

Daisies Vase Pattern   **Enlarge 200%**

A   A

9
project

How do I paint a one-stroke daisy using a shader paintbrush?

A shader paintbrush yields harder edges on the daisy petals, dictating a bold statement about this hurricane that is followed by dark-colored leaves and grapes.

What You Need to Get Started:

Disposable palette or foam plate
Glass hurricane
Glaze paint: clear gloss
Permenamel paints: light burgundy; goldenrod; green; hunter green; red; white
Round paintbrush: #5
Script liner paint brush: #1
Shader paintbrush: #10
Surface conditioner
Tracing paper
Transparent tape

Daisy Hurricane

Here's How:
Note: Refer to Strokework Techniques on pages 19–27.

1. Refer to Preparing the Surface on page 19. Apply a coat of surface conditioner onto glass.

2. Enlarge Daisy Hurricane Pattern at right. Tape photocopy inside hurricane.

3. Using shader paintbrush loaded with white, paint one-stroke daisy petals.

4. Using round paintbrush loaded with goldenrod, tap in daisy centers. While still wet, add light burgundy to lower right of each center and white to upper left of each center. Allow to dry.

5. Using shader paintbrush side-loaded with hunter green, float shading around edges of each center.

Enlarge 135%

Daisy Hurricane Pattern

6. Using handle end of paintbrush and alternating red and burgundy, paint dots for grapes.

7. Using shader paintbrush double-loaded with green and hunter green, paint leaves with combination of an s-stroke and a one-stroke.

8. Using script liner paintbrush loaded with green and hunter green, paint one-stroke leaves and filler strokes.

9. Allow paint to cure for 10 days before using.

10 project

What You Need to Get Started:

Chalk-based paper
Disposable palette or foam plate
Glaze paint: clear gloss
Liner paintbrush: #1
Paper towels
Permenamel paints: black; brown; light burgundy; goldenrod; green; hunter green; ivory; red; burnt sienna
Script liner paintbrush: #1
Sea sponge
Shader paintbrushes: #4; #8; #10
Surface conditioner
Whiteware cup, saucer, teapot

The entire surface of each of these whiteware pieces was sponge-painted with a sea sponge and two shades of paint. The apple and vine designs were painted directly over the sponging.

Apple Orchard Tea Set

Here's How:
Note: Refer to Strokework Techniques on pages 19–27.

1. Refer to Preparing the Surface on page 19. Apply a coat of surface conditioner onto each piece.

2. Place sea sponge in water. Blot water from sponge onto paper towel so sponge is merely damp. Using sponge loaded with ivory, sponge outside of cup, saucer, and teapot. Allow to dry.

3. Apply second coat of ivory and while still wet, lightly sponge on a coat of goldenrod. Allow to dry.

4. Enlarge Apple Pattern on opposite page. Using chalk-based paper, transfer photocopied pattern onto side of teapot and cup.

5. Using #8 shader paintbrush loaded with red, base-coat apple. Allow to dry. Apply second coat of red.

6. Using #10 shader paintbrush side-loaded with light burgundy, float shading on apple.

7. Using #10 shader paintbrush side-loaded with goldenrod, float a highlight on apple.

8. Using #10 shader paintbrush side-loaded with ivory, float a second highlight on apple.

9. Using liner paintbrush loaded with burnt sienna, paint stem.

10. Enlarge Plate Vine Pattern and Teapot Vine Pattern on opposite page. Using chalk-based paper, transfer patterns around edge of plate and teapot lid.

11. Using #8 shader paintbrush side-loaded with black, float shading on stem.

12. Using #8 shader paintbrush loaded with green, base-coat leaves.

13. Using #8 shader paintbrush side-loaded with hunter green, float shading on leaves.

14. Using #10 shader paintbrush side-loaded with burnt sienna, float under apples to form a base line.

15. Using liner paintbrush loaded with black, outline entire design.

16. Using script liner loaded with brown, paint vine around lid of teapot and rim of saucer. Repeat with black.

17. Using #4 shader paintbrush double-loaded with green and hunter green stroke on leaves of vine.

18. Using liner paintbrush loaded with black, line all leaves.

19. Using #8 shader paintbrush double-loaded with red and light burgundy, paint checks. Allow to dry.

20. Using #10 shader paintbrush, evenly apply two coats of glaze over entire surface of each piece. Allow to dry between coats.

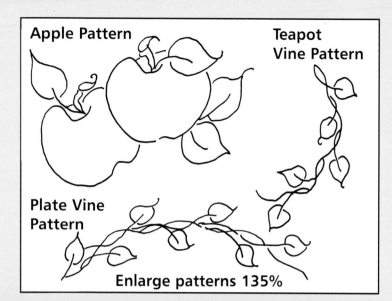

Apple Pattern

Teapot Vine Pattern

Plate Vine Pattern

Enlarge patterns 135%

How do I paint a motif
on a solid-colored background?

What You Need
to Get Started:

Clock face
Clock works kit
Compressed
  sponge
Craft scissors
Dark graphite
  paper
Disposable palette
  or foam plate
Electric drill with
  $5/16$"-dia. masonry
  bit
Glaze paint: clear
  gloss
Hot-glue gun and
  glue sticks
Masking tape
Paper towels
Pencil
Permanent mark-
  ing pen: black
Permenamel
  paints: black;
  navy blue; coral;
  gray; green; red;
  tangerine; white;
  yellow
Porcelain plate:
  white, 10"-dia.
Porcelain utensil
  holder: white
Round paint-
  brushes: #3; #5
Ruler
Shader paintbrush:
  #10
Silicone adhesive
Sponge paintbrush
Stylus
Surface conditioner
Tracing paper
Wash paintbrush:
  $3/4$"

It is important to know how to transfer a design onto a background that has already been painted with a solid color. Dark graphite paper is essential to successful transfers.

Bunny Clock & Utensil Holder
Photograph on page 86.

Here's How:
Note: Refer to Strokework Techniques on pages 19–27. Wear safety glasses when using power tools.

1. Using ruler and permanent marking pen, mark center of plate on front and back.

2. To prevent plate from chipping or cracking when drilling, turn plate face down. Apply two pieces of masking tape in a crisscross fashion, intersecting at drilling point. Repeat taping process several times.

3. Turn plate over. Using glue gun, run a circle of glue approximately ½" from center around dot.

4. Carefully drill hole in center of plate to accommodate clock works. Remove all tape and glue.

5. Refer to Preparing the Surface on page 19. Apply a coat of surface conditioner onto each piece.

6. Apply silicone adhesive to back side of clock face. Center and press face on front of plate. Following manufacturer's instructions, allow to dry.

7. Using wash paintbrush loaded with navy blue, base-coat outer rim of plate and bottom section of utensil holder. Allow to dry and repeat for second coat.

8. Using pencil, trace Bunny Pattern on opposite page onto tracing paper. Using dark graphite paper, transfer traced pattern onto front of plate and utensil holder.

9. Using shader paintbrush loaded with gray, paint bunnies.

10. Using shader paintbrush side-loaded with white, float a highlight on bunnies.

11. Using #3 round paintbrush loaded with black, paint laydowns for eyes.

12. Using #3 round paintbrush loaded with coral, paint laydowns for noses.

13. Using stylus loaded with white, paint "sparkle" dots on eyes.

14. Using pencil, trace Carrot Pattern, and Circle Pattern on opposite page

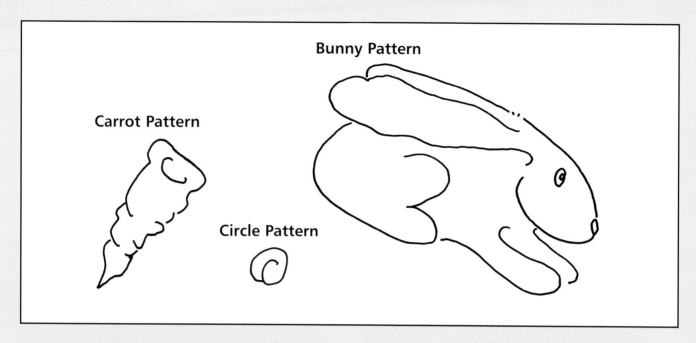

Bunny Pattern

Carrot Pattern

Circle Pattern

onto tracing paper. Cut out traced patterns and trace onto sponge. Using scissors, cut shapes from sponge. Cut ½" square from sponge.

15. Place shapes in water and allow to puff up. Blot water from sponges onto paper towel so sponges are merely damp. Set aside.

16. Refer to Technique 4 Step 4 on page 36. Load carrot sponge with tangerine.

17. Press carrot onto plate and utensil holder, positioning tip near feet of bunny. Allow to dry. Rinse sponge with clean water and blot dry.

18. Repeat Steps 17–18, double-loading sponge with yellow on one edge and red on the other edge and pressing second image directly over first.

19. Pour a small amount of green and yellow paints on palette. Side-load one edge of circle sponge with green and the opposite edge with yellow. Blot 3–4 times on another part of palette until sponge is evenly loaded with paint. Repeat if more paint is needed. Note: When sponge is completely loaded, carefully start applying the design.

20. Press circle several times onto plate and utensil holder at rounded end of carrot and allow to dry. Rinse sponge with clean water and blot dry.

21. Using #3 round paintbrush loaded with yellow, paint three one-strokes between bunny and carrot.

22. Pour a small amount of yellow, red, and tangerine paints on palette. Dip square sponge in yellow and blot 3–4 times on another part of palette until sponge is evenly loaded with paint. Side-load one edge of square sponge with red and the opposite edge with tangerine. Repeat if more paint is needed.

23. Press square onto plate evenly spacing along bottom edge of navy blue and onto utensil holder evenly spacing along top edge of navy blue and allow to dry. Rinse sponge with clean water and blot dry.

24. Using #3 round paintbrush loaded with navy blue, paint ribbon along checkered borders.

25. Using handle end of paintbrush loaded with navy blue, randomly paint dots around white sections of plate and utensil holder.

26. Using #5 round paintbrush, double-loaded with tangerine and yellow, paint three laydowns on edges of clock face at 3, 6, 9, and 12.

27. Using sponge paintbrush loaded with red, paint outside edge of plate.

28. Using sponge paintbrush loaded with navy blue, paint outside edge of utensil holder.

29. Using permanent marking pen, outline bun-nies and carrots, and add squiggly lines along borders.

30. Using wash paintbrush, evenly apply two coats of glaze over entire surface of each piece. Allow to dry between coats.

31. Following manufacturer's instructions, insert clock works.

How do I create a design with laydowns and one-strokes?

It is easy to create an entire design with one or two paint strokes. The design is accented by a solid yellow background. You will be using the reverse-painting technique on the plate.

What You Need to Get Started:

Cosmetic sponges
Disposable palette
  or foam plate
Glass goblets (2),
  plate
Glaze paint: clear
  gloss
Liner paintbrush:
  #1
Permenamel
  paints: blue;
  fuchsia; green;
  yellow
Round paintbrush:
  #3
Shader paintbrush:
  #12
Surface conditioner
Transparent tape

Garden of Blossoms
Photographs on pages 88–89.

Here's How:
Note: Refer to Strokework Techniques on pages 19–27.

1. Refer to Preparing the Surface on page 19. Apply a coat of surface conditioner onto each piece.

2. Refer to Technique 8 Step 2 on page 45. Apply tape around large goblet 1¼" from rim.

3. Refer to Technique 8 Step 3 on page 45. Base-coat glass above tape with yellow.

4. Using round paintbrush heavily loaded with blue, paint four laydowns per flower. Note: Vary placement of every other flower along bottom of yellow, so flowers are half on yellow and half on clear glass. The remaining flowers are randomly placed depending on your surface and on how many or how few you wish to use.

5. Using round paintbrush loaded with fuchsia, paint a laydown for each flower center.

6. Using round paintbrush heavily loaded with green, paint a laydown for each leaf around flowers.

7. Using liner paintbrush loaded with green, paint one-stroke leaves to fill in design.

8. Apply tape around small goblet ¾" from rim.

9. Using a piece of cosmetic sponge loaded with yellow, base-coat below tape. Allow to dry and repeat for second coat. Remove tape immediately after applying last coat.

10. Repeat Steps 4–7 alternating flowers and one-stroke leaves around top edge of yellow, half on yellow and half on clear glass. Randomly paint flowers and leaves over remaining yellow area of goblet.

11. Repeat Steps 4–7 to randomly paint flowers and leaves over underside of outer rim of plate. Paint a double row of one-strokes around center. Allow to dry.

12. Using a piece of cosmetic sponge loaded with yellow, base-coat outer rim of plate (over flowers and leaves). Allow to dry and repeat for second coat.

13. Using shader paintbrush, evenly apply two coats of glaze over painted areas of each piece. Allow to dry between coats.

designed by Terri Newberry

designed by Donna Young

designed by Terri Newberry

designed by Marta Bacon

designed by J-Crafts

designed by Nikki St. Mary

Section 4: *gallery of artists*

designed by Donna Young

designed by Nikki St. Mary

Terri Newberry has lived in beautiful Washington state her entire life. She started out in Bremerton, lived in Aberdeen for 20 years, and currently resides in Shelton.

Over the years, Terri has expressed creativity in many forms—floral arranging, crafts, cooking, and gardening. Painting is a relatively new outlet for her fascination with color. "I've always been in such awe of the beauty of nature, such as a rainbow," she says. "I love how the colors all melt together, but are still distinct."

Her studio is named "Le Coeur de Joie" (pronounced le coor de jwa). It is French for "heart of joy." She chose this name as a constant reminder of how important it is to be happy, no matter what arises.

Terri's husband Lantz has been a strong support in her endeavor. She has been blessed with two children, Ambria and Chayce, as well as two step-children, Heather and Cameron. 1999 gave her new inspiration when her beautiful grandson Taylor was born.

designed by Terri Newberry

designed by Terri Newberry

designed by Terri Newberry

designed by Terri Newberry

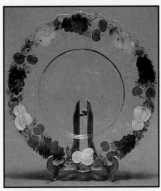

designed by Terri Newberry

designed by Terri Newberry

designed by Terri Newberry

designed by Terri Newberry

designed by Terri Newberry

designed by Terri Newberry

designed by Terri Newberry

designed by Terri Newberry

designed by Terri Newberry

designed by Terri Newberry

designed by Terri Newberry

J-Crafts Handpainted Glass is a small "cottage industry" run by June Coope and Jacqui Redden. All of their glassware is done from home and produced in small quantities, keeping them as unique as possible.

J-Crafts began in 1997 as a hobby—the two women were painting on jam jars to make summer night lights. Soon they were crafting small glass pieces as gifts for family and friends.

Today, June and Jacqui hand-paint on almost any type of glassware, from glasses to vases, bowls to mirrors, in a wide variety of vibrant and beautiful colors and designs. Both women are self-taught in the art of glass painting and have read numerous books on the subject. Through experimentation with new ideas and colors, they are able to create one-of-a-kind pieces.

Although J-Crafts is far from developing into a business, it has gone quite a ways beyond being just a hobby. Their glass can be found for sale in local shops, craft fairs held throughout the year, and as a recent addition, at The Coach House Gift Centre at Lea, Derbyshire, England.

June and Jacqui have participated in numerous craft fairs since they began painting on glass. They have done one local exhibition and plan to display their glass in a local library in the near future.

In January of 2000, J-Crafts was invited to give a demonstration for a local chapter of Women's Institute Group. This included a hands-on experience for members of the group, which proved to be a huge success enjoyed by all.

designed by J-Crafts

designed by J-Crafts

designed by J-Crafts

designed by J-Crafts

designed by J-Crafts

99

designed by J-Crafts

designed by J-Crafts

designed by Nikki St. Mary

Though it wasn't intentional, **Nikki St. Mary** is the artist, owner, and manager of Geez Louise Artware and she couldn't be happier about it.

What originally began as a creative way to pass the time during the very long Adirondack Mountain winters, turned into a growing business.

After finding that people were drawn to the whimsical designs at regional art and craft shows, she boldly launched the website, www.geez-louise.com in October 1999.

With incredible encouragement and support of family and friends, Geez Louise is doing business all over the world. Nikki does however, continue to take her wares on the road throughout the Northeast so she can get her "people fix."

designed by Nikki St. Mary

designed by Nikki St. Mary

designed by Nikki St. Mary

designed by Nikki St. Mary

Donna Young, glass and tile artist, was born at Mercer Island, Washington, in 1954 and has lived in Bend, Oregon, since 1996.

"I was formally schooled as a graphic illustrator and supported myself in this field as well as having numerous Seattle exhibitions as a fine artist. My style and creativity eventually evolved to kiln work in glass and tile. I enjoy the concept that my art will be appreciated functionally as well as aesthetically."

designed by Donna Young

designed by Donna Young

106

designed by Donna Young

designed by Donna Young

107

designed by Donna Young

designed by Donna Young

designed by Donna Young

Marta says that most people buy her lamps for their beauty rather than their function. She believes the lamps remind people of a grandmother's home or other place that holds special memories. Her work is featured in homes all over the world.

Work on the lamps may take anywhere from one week to two months depending on the detail of the design and Marta's schedule. "Even though I work every day," she explains. "It can take a while to finish a piece because it is all done by hand. I am very fortunate because I love this work and it is something special to a lot of people."

Marta Bacon is from the new generation of glass artists, carrying on the tradition of painters from the Victorian era.

Born in 1954 in Los Angeles, California, Marta earned an Associate of Arts degree from Fullerton College. She continues to take college-level art classes to help her grow as an artist.

Presently, in addition to creating commissioned pieces, Marta teaches painting for the North Orange County Community College district to at least 80 students on a weekly basis.

"My canvas is glass," says Marta. "For me it is the best of both worlds. I get the translucent look of watercolors, yet the paint moves like oil."

Marta paints flowers or other scenes on hand-blown opal-glass globes. Her painting is then fired at least three times so it becomes a permanent part of the glass. Each piece of art is an original heirloom, signed by Marta.

designed by Marta Bacon

Metric equivalency chart

mm-millimetres cm-centimetres
inches to millimetres and centimetres

inches	mm	cm	inches	cm	inches	cm
⅛	3	0.3	9	22.9	30	76.2
¼	6	0.6	10	25.4	31	78.7
⅜	10	1.0	11	27.9	32	81.3
½	13	1.3	12	30.5	33	83.8
⅝	16	1.6	13	33.0	34	86.4
¾	19	1.9	14	35.6	35	88.9
⅞	22	2.2	15	38.1	36	91.4
1	25	2.5	16	40.6	37	94.0
1¼	32	3.2	17	43.2	38	96.5
1½	38	3.8	18	45.7	39	99.1
1¾	44	4.4	19	48.3	40	101.6
2	51	5.1	20	50.8	41	104.1
2½	64	6.4	21	53.3	42	106.7
3	76	7.6	22	55.9	43	109.2
3½	89	8.9	23	58.4	44	111.8
4	102	10.2	24	61.0	45	114.3
4½	114	11.4	25	63.5	46	116.8
5	127	12.7	26	66.0	47	119.4
6	152	15.2	27	68.6	48	121.9
7	178	17.8	28	71.1	49	124.5
8	203	20.3	29	73.7	50	127.0

yards to metres

yards	metres	yards	metres	yards	metres	yards	metres	yards	metres
⅛	0.11	2⅛	1.94	4⅛	3.77	6⅛	5.60	8⅛	7.43
¼	0.23	2¼	2.06	4¼	3.89	6¼	5.72	8¼	7.54
⅜	0.34	2⅜	2.17	4⅜	4.00	6⅜	5.83	8⅜	7.66
½	0.46	2½	2.29	4½	4.11	6½	5.94	8½	7.77
⅝	0.57	2⅝	2.40	4⅝	4.23	6⅝	6.06	8⅝	7.89
¾	0.69	2¾	2.51	4¾	4.34	6¾	6.17	8¾	8.00
⅞	0.80	2⅞	2.63	4⅞	4.46	6⅞	6.29	8⅞	8.12
1	0.91	3	2.74	5	4.57	7	6.40	9	8.23
1⅛	1.03	3⅛	2.86	5⅛	4.69	7⅛	6.52	9⅛	8.34
1¼	1.14	3¼	2.97	5¼	4.80	7¼	6.63	9¼	8.46
1⅜	1.26	3⅜	3.09	5⅜	4.91	7⅜	6.74	9⅜	8.57
1½	1.37	3½	3.20	5½	5.03	7½	6.86	9½	8.69
1⅝	1.49	3⅝	3.31	5⅝	5.14	7⅝	6.97	9⅝	8.80
1¾	1.60	3¾	3.43	5¾	5.26	7¾	7.09	9¾	8.92
1⅞	1.71	3⅞	3.54	5⅞	5.37	7⅞	7.20	9⅞	9.03
2	1.83	4	3.66	6	5.49	8	7.32	10	9.14

Index

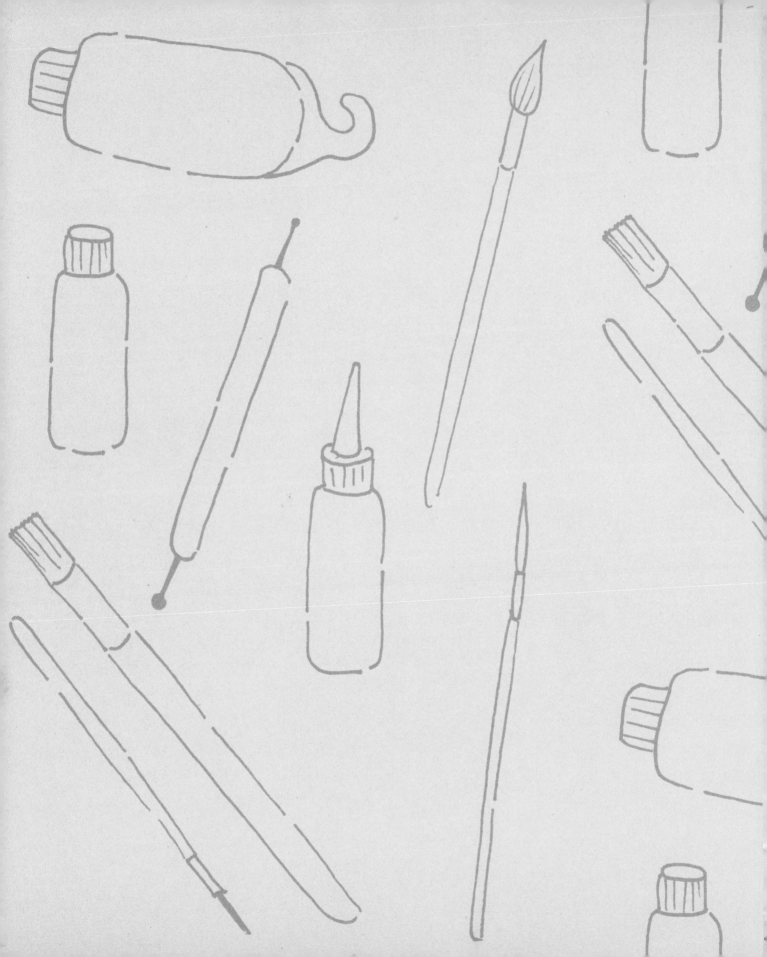